BEING INVISIBLE:
Men of Colour Talk About
Love, Life, and Fatherhood

By

Kenny Harry

Conscious Dreams
PUBLISHING

First Printed in United Kingdom 2021

Published by Conscious Dreams Publishing

Edited by Elise Abram and Daniella Blechner

Cover Design by Justina Misdemeanour
www.justarmisdemeanor.co.uk

Typeset by Oksana Kosovan

www.consciousdreamspublishing.com

@consciousdreamspublishing

ISBN: 978-1-913674-86-1

Dedication

To my father Titus Harry, my niece Nadine, family and friends we have lost in our life's journey.

Henry Scott's poem states, 'death is nothing at all... I have only slipped away into the next room... I am but waiting for you, for an interval... how we shall laugh at the trouble of parting when we meet again.'

Contents

Preface and Acknowledgements

This is my first book, and it is fair to say it has taken much longer than I expected, give or take a few years. I had no idea how long writing this book would take or the bumps and bruises I would encounter along the way.

My original thought was to compile a short, six-chapter book that would represent the thoughts, feelings, and experiences of fatherhood in the UK. However, the more I listened to fathers, the more issues surfaced, and the thicker the book became. There is no doubt the book changed from what I thought it would be to what the fathers decided it would be. For this, I do not apologise, as it was a rare opportunity to speak to fathers who were more than willing to talk about issues they had long wanted to air but had little opportunity to do so.

So, I feel a sense of pride and achievement that I was accepted and allowed to be inquisitive, explore, and at times, find answers to dilemmas that men have, such as how to balance our lives' experiences, living in the UK and juggling our responsibilities towards our families. What I hope we have learned on this long journey is that, as individuals, we do not have the answers, but as a group of fathers, we are stronger in our endeavours when we share our ideas to find some of life's answers – a blueprint to fatherhood.

A big indebtedness goes to all those fathers who grappled with some of the difficult and uncomfortable topics within this book. It meant sometimes having to share their emotions and personal lives with others, which proved invaluable along the way when it came to validating and enriching the choices of the chapters. Fathers – such as Michael Samuels, Spencer Isaac, Tony Josiah, Benjamin Prince, Leon James, Justine Moore – I can never repay you. Your words and insights are spread throughout my book, and I hope that when you read the book, it will bring a smile to your face. Your thoughts and views will always be with me.

I have to thank the strength of Wendy Laviniere, Denise Cassell, Janet Smith and my niece Nadine, who understood the importance of my completing this book and who continually pushed me to do so, no matter what! The inner strength of these women came to the fore to push me to the finish line. Justin's resourcefulness, whose contacts know no bounds, provided me with the missing jigsaw puzzle piece to my book: grandfathers. To Marilyn, the mother of my children, who had to endure my constant typing at all hours of the day and night for years, and my super talented children, Aaliyah and Terrel, of whom I am so proud because of their strength of character, in making their way in the world and the respect they show towards their elders and all they meet; it melts my old heart. They inspire me to stretch the boundaries of my mind to develop further and try to be a good role model. To Omari, Nikel, and Tricia Isaac, who provided me with creative ideas and energy when I struggled to piece together the names and contents of the chapters: the chapter entitled 'My Money, Your Money, and Our Money' was one of the many ideas they shared with me. To the talented artist Justina Misdemeanour who created my book cover, and to Daniella Blechner, my publisher and mentor who navigated me through the maze of publishing my book and having to put up with my procrastinating!

My parents, Isla and Titus Harry, God rest his soul, who provided us all with love, food in our bellies, a routine, a sense of humility, the importance of family, and how to keep a cool head whilst those around us lose theirs.

Last but by no means least, my brothers and sisters, Mary, Irene, Linda, Hillius, James, Eileen, and Roy: although some of us live close by and we are able to get together as much as we can to enjoy each other's company, some of us are far away, yet our love for each other when we meet knows no bounds. I do not know how our parents were able to guide and provide for us all over the years, but if I can do half as good a job as my parents, I will be happy!

I sincerely hope that fathers across the UK and beyond will find some commonality and answers in the experience of the fathers in this book, and if you have that spear of energy, don't be afraid to invite to meet with other fathers. I have learned so much about myself and the joys and perils of fatherhood that I would not replace my experience for the world. I have been in a privileged position writing this book, and I can honestly say that I am a better person for it. You will be surprised how many fathers are itching to sit down, talk with other fathers, and not have to go through the bravado of showing off to prove their masculinity. The conversations are about our lives as fathers and how this has an impact on our everyday life and relationships. If there is motivation, these fathers – whether from a small or large group – will continue to meet long after this book has gathered dust.

Introduction – Being Invisible

*"Beginnings are usually scary, and endings are usually sad; but it's
everything in between that makes it all worth living."*
– Bob Marley

We are the invisible fathers who go about our daily duties, unnoticed
by society. You will not see us in newspapers or magazines or on TV
programmes. In fact, you may not know that we exist. Why? Because no
one really wants to know us, our dreams, our challenges, our experiences,
or our heartaches. Isn't being a father one of the many roles we have in
everyday life? Aren't we just normal human beings like everyone else with
the same challenges life throws at us?

What marks us out as being different from other fathers in Britain is
that we are men of colour. Although that should not matter, we frequently
receive negative publicity rather than positive. The media seems to be apt
at finding negative representations of fathers rather than praising those of
us who are responsible who work and look after our children. Believe me
when I say that I have met many on my four-year journey whilst writing
this book who are angry at being represented in the media as uncaring,
selfish, womanising players, uneducated, criminally minded, lacking
discipline, lacking ambition, and most of all, lacking any financial or moral
responsibility towards their children and family units.

This book is about the experiences of fathers of colour living in modern-
day Britain. On the whole, the fathers are like most other fathers in Britain,
living either with their wives/partners and children, separated and co-
parenting, or estranged from their children. However, their experiences
with manhood and fatherhood have been shaped by two contrasting

cultures – Caribbean or African and British – so this book takes an in-depth look at how these cultures affect their maleness, parenting skills, and relationships.

This book brings together fathers who openly talk about their innermost fears surrounding their parenting styles, family relationships, views on bringing up children, attitudes towards education and finances, and relationships with the world of work; the growing number of partners/wives earning more than their male counterparts and the effects on their relationships; how, as men, we deal with our emotions; why we struggle to show public affection to our partners; and fathers who have separated from their families and the impact on their well-being.

At times, you will laugh at their experiences of growing up in Britain, their love affairs with the national game of football, and the lengths they will go to watch a match, or how they struggle to admit to their partners about being wrong. On other occasions, you will feel the pain when some of the fathers recall the discipline they endured from their disciplinarian fathers and how this has affected their relationships and parenting skills, how, during boyhood and teenage hood, they were programmed to distance themselves from having emotions as 'big boys don't cry', or trying to belong in a country that can, at times, be hostile towards them, leading to a feeling of not belonging.

My book also has chapters that bring together a cross-generational view of fatherhood. Children, teenagers, grandfathers, and of course, fathers all give their views to gauge different perceptions of fatherhood from the past to the present. The children's views are clear as to what they like and dislike about their fathers, and it makes for interesting reading!

So, we provide a lot of ideas from fathers who have been there about how to deal with the most common scenarios your sons and daughters will come across. We were able to obtain the views of grandfathers who provided us with a unique insight into their African and Caribbean upbringing, how this influenced their fathering methods at the time (1950-1970s), and how their grown-up children are coping with modern-day expectations towards parenting. Has parenting in modern-day Britain changed for the good or for the worse is one of the many questions they tackle?

Most of all, the fatherhood groups who helped me compile this book reach out to fathers of all persuasions to share their experiences, ideas, and methods to become even better fathers than we are today. You will find that whatever your culture or nationality, fatherhood has certain common traits within its masculine make-up and these traits can influence us as fathers. For instance, why are sports so important to men? Why do some men cook and others do not? Why do we have to be near death before we will see a doctor? Why do we have difficulty admitting we are lost whilst driving and asking for directions and/or help? How do we teach our sons through our experiences in Britain about how to be responsible men for their families, and what messages are we transmitting to our daughters about our attitudes towards women via our behaviours towards our partners or wives?

The emphasis of the book is on understanding ourselves as men and the complexities of living in Britain so we can teach our sons the survival skills needed to succeed in society, providing them with a good role model or blueprint to ensure we bring them up right so they can stay safe in a hostile environment. The journey has been long, and at times, the debates heated. However, what emerged from these differences are strong friendships based on mutual respect and a sense that we are finally able to talk. We hope this book, contributed to and for fathers, is filled with ideas that will enable you to gain a generational overview of fatherhood and teach you new approaches to modern-day parenting.

What the fathers have come to realise – and we hope you do, too – is that irrelevant of whether you agree with the contents of the book, it will get you thinking about your important role as a father and a lover and not to be afraid to talk when the time arises. We hope you, too, can start your own fatherhood groups in your areas because, as fathers, we have experienced so much and have a lot to say. You just have to find the venue and time in your hectic lives to sit down and talk. As the introductory quotation states, it's what we do between being born and death that counts the most, so by getting together and sharing your ideas you will learn new methods in your quest to be the best father you can possibly be.

Goodbye to the Belt: Modern-day Approaches to Disciplining Children

Childhood stories from the past

Many fathers speak about the method of discipline their fathers used against them whilst growing up. What is clear from the discussions with fathers in which I either participated or observed is that, as boys, we learned to accept the authority of our fathers without question. A study of 29 families by the Joseph Rowntree Foundation into parenting beliefs and practices (White British, Black African, Black Caribbean, and Pakistani) concluded that although men's roles within families is being transformed, some traditional roles still persist amongst certain groups. For instance, families' attitudes towards men providing a 'good fathering' role is linked to disciplining children. The big question for us fathers is to what extent have our childhood experiences of discipline affected how we discipline our children today? I had no trouble finding fathers from all socio-economic groups in areas across the country that were willing to talk about their childhood experiences. On the next few pages are comments from fathers during an interview.

> **Trevor:** 'To this day, if I don't smile, I would cry. I was unruly and arrogant and needed someone to keep me in check. I remember doing so many things, getting into trouble, without thinking of the consequences. My dad was just hard, and I was frightened of him because when he got vexed (angry) he went to war with his belt. He always seemed to know exactly where to hit us he and his two other brothers to get maximum pain. The beatings were not nice; not nice at all.'

The younger, second-generation fathers in the group who had elder brothers and sisters had a mixed experience when it came to discipline from their first-generation fathers. Being the younger children in the families, they seemed to have been spared Dad's notorious belt beatings compared

16

to their older brothers because their fathers seemed to have mellowed as they aged. However, the question a lot of these fathers – who were not as fortunate as their younger siblings – want to ask their fathers but could not find the courage to do so: why, knowing the pain they'd endured from their fathers' beatings as children, did they inflict the same belt beatings against them? As a second-generation father eloquently explained:

> **Adrian:** 'If my dad hated Granddad for what he'd done to him, why do the same to me? It doesn't make sense – don't you think he would say, "I'm not going to beat my children like I was?" He had a distant relationship with his father and so do we.'

> **Father:** 'My dad was something else. I swear he used to think of ways to punish us just for the sake of it. A few times, he just threw a bucket of water on us whilst we were in bed because we had trouble getting up in the morning. I'm telling you, although the water wasn't ice cold, it might as well have been because, in bed, you are so warm. It shocks me to the core when I think about it as an adult. Imagine that – a bucket of cold water! I would never, never do that to my kids. There are other ways to deal with it.'

Maybe surprisingly, but not uncommon, some fathers I've met viewed their father's discipline differently.

> **Trevor:** 'I know some of you won't agree with what I am saying, but the beatings from my dad made sure I never made the same mistake again. I stayed correct. I had to think before I caused mischief because what would Dad find to hit me with this time. You see, the problem with kids nowadays is that they do not fear their parents because parents want to be their friends, and before you know it,

the kids run the house. I'm telling you, that's not happening in my house, no way, over my dead body.' He meant it, too!

What seems apparent in all the fathers with whom I have spoken is their fathers' punishments towards them, which were swift, hard, and at times, merciless. One father became very animated whilst explaining having to run down the street as his dad whipped him with his belt. The group wanted to know how he could smile whilst talking about such a traumatic experience. Here lies the dilemma because attitudes towards parenting and disciplining children have changed considerably from when these fathers were young in the late 1960s, 1970s, and 1980s. Having experienced the traditional type of discipline with the belt from our fathers, we now live in a modern-day society where such physical chastisement is unacceptable.

UK statistics on physical punishment
To give you a sense and an overview of the physical punishment of children in the UK, here are some research statistics.[1] So, just how common is physical punishment used by parents against their children in Britain, and what do these statistics tell us about our attitudes towards punishing children?

- 90% of parents admit to using physical punishment at some time
- 80% admit to using it within the last year
- 48% of 4-year-olds are hit at least once a week
- 35% of 7-year-olds are hit at least once a week
- Only 11% of children think smacking is okay, and then, only for older children

---

1   Davies, 2006

Davies goes on to conclude that it is illegal to assault an adult or animal, but it is within the law to reasonably punish your children. Children do not have the same protection as animals, so common assaults from parents or a significant adult is possible.

The discussion with different individual fathers and groups turned into an amazing insight into the tension between old and new methods of disciplining children in the UK. As mentioned previously, the big question for us fathers is to what extent have our childhood experiences of discipline affected how we discipline our children today? So, let's look at the 'types' of fathers I found on my journey.

The 'disciplinarian' and the 'reasoned' father

When talking to fathers, it was clear that to simplify the grouping of fathers, two opposing camps on disciplining children existed. The traditional or 'disciplinarian' father's style of punishment was characterised by limited verbal warnings. 'If you can't hear, you must feel' is a time-honoured saying, and some fathers still use this saying to get their children to stop misbehaving.

> **Father:** 'I use the saying all the time, so when I say stop, I mean it. It is a powerful warning that ensures the children understand right from wrong.'

The group also identified a more modern approach I call the 'reasoned' discipline approach, whereby the fathers take the time to communicate and think about how to punish or 'sanction' their children without reverting to physical chastisement. This approach seems to involve parent's taking away the child's privileges for a given period of time, depending on the age of the child and the seriousness of what the child has done. Both approaches caused quite heated debates amongst the two opposing camps.

The 'disciplinarian' fathers believed 'sanctioning' children by talking and reasoning with them was too soft an option for bringing up children. They believed this approach to discipline is making children too soft for the unforgiving world in which we live, and it allows them to take psychological control within the home, ultimately undermining their parental authority. These fathers cited the increasing incidents of teenagers' 'happy slapping' adults in the community, general rudeness towards adults, indiscriminate muggings towards the elderly in particular, the increase in violence and fatalities, and gang membership as indicators of teenagers' running the streets and being in charge of adults rather than the other way round when they were growing up.

> **Delroy:** 'You see, this is the problem: parents nowadays have become too soft, and teenagers run the streets. Adults on the streets are scared to tell them off because they are frightened those kids will slag them off or beat them up. You must have seen that situation on the bus, in the park, and at shops where adults just turn a blind eye rather than get involved. That is why children need strong discipline from day one. Yeah, I am not talking about beating your child to death – that is just wicked. You can call me a disciplinarian if you like that label, but that's not a bad thing. I'm getting the sense that's how it's being seen tonight, but I'd bet you my teenagers right now are having fun but on the whole, behaving because they know I will come down hard on them if they don't.'

The rationale behind the 'disciplinarian' fathers in the group goes back generations. These 'disciplinarian' fathers learned via their fathers that discipline should be impartial and no favouritism should be shown to any child as keeping them in check is a man's role. The belt became a symbol of the alpha-male power over their male offspring as a method of keeping them in line and understanding their low pecking order within the family unit. Similarly, in the animal kingdom, you will see male lions play fighting with their offspring; however, there is a serious side to the play fighting. This is how the male lion shows the young male cub that Dad is stronger than him, but if the male cub wants to challenge his father's authority, he is likely to be taught a brutal lesson in rough play. Of course, we are not in the animal kingdom, and we use this as an example to show that these fathers are the alpha-males, and through their show of strength, they lay the boundaries of what is considered right or wrong within the household. Their judgements are final, and their punishments are swift if you cross the rules of the house. In short, they are in charge.

The belt symbolises a father's power, the presence of authority over his children, and in particular, his son, to chastise him and remain in charge until the time comes for his son to stand on his own two feet. As the lion prepares his cubs for the unforgiving animal world, so does the 'disciplinarian' father prepare his son for the tough world that lies ahead of him as a young Black male. As a part of a minority group in Britain, these fathers believe they are teaching their sons the harshness of life. The fathers' rationale is if their sons can survive their tough upbringing, their jobs are complete in raising their sons to respect their elders, and in particular, respect themselves and authority. A growing number of fathers have attributed the decline in teenage discipline within society to the decline in parents using effective chastisement, and the only way to regain control is to introduce stronger disciplinary methods.

On the other side of the argument are the fathers, who, as children, were also beaten with a belt by their fathers, but they have made the conscious decision not to duplicate their 'disciplinarian' dads' approaches to bringing up their children, believing that the world of parenting has moved on, and they also needed to. A few fathers initially admitted to hitting their children but decided that approach did not sit comfortably with them.

Dwayne: 'Seeing my son's shock and tears made me feel guilty. He had really got into trouble, and I just exploded. Beating my son was more out of frustration on my part than about what he had actually done. I vowed never to hit my son like that again. It reminded me of the beats I got from my dad, and I didn't want to be like him. Although I didn't get beats that many times compared to some guys, I know it still sticks with me because, you know, in this day and age, it would be seen as child abuse. So, I invested time by reading books and talking to friends to learn different methods for disciplining my son. I decided to use, I suppose, what the group is calling the "reasoned" approach to punishment. I don't really like the definition, but I'm not bothered by giving it a name, and it just seems a fairer approach to me as I don't want my son hating me.'

Another father told a profound story to the group:

Steve: 'Our father beat me and my brother with the belt, bamboo sticks, shoes, and tree branches, in fact, anything he could get his hands on. At times, he would just lose it, swinging wildly at us, and although we screamed, asking him to stop, he carried on. My brother was older than me and was supposed to control me, so he got extra beats if I didn't behave. After he had finished beating us, the room was a mess, like a hurricane had hit it. We both swore never to beat our own children like that, and to this day, we have not.'

Steve's childhood experience led to feelings of being an ineffective disciplinarian towards his children. He knew he did not want to use his father's methods, but he was unsure as to which methods to use. He felt he was losing control of his household by his inaction over finding other methods to discipline his children.

I find that fathers attend groups for various reasons, some to share their experience of being a father whilst others are in search of new ideas to improve their parenting. Steve attended the group to find out the latter, to reverse the pattern into which he had fallen. He wanted to be a more effective father and instil boundaries rather than revert back to what he had experienced as a child from his dad. He told the group a touching story about his son at school and the impact of his childhood upbringing on their relationship.

Steve's 12-year-old son was being bullied at school, and Steve and his wife met with the headteacher to resolve the situation. His wife provided their son with emotional support by talking to him and reassuring him that it was not his fault. When his wife asked him in front of his son to add a few words, he could not, and he became angry with her for 'putting him on the spot'. He explained that he found it difficult to share his partner's emotional connection because of his own upbringing.

Steve's father was a disciplinarian and a man of a few words. His father worked long hours and lacked patience, so contact with his father was limited. In fact, the majority of contact his siblings had with their father was during one of the many beatings. Their father would use almost anything at hand with which to hit him and his siblings. He grew up frightened and distant from his dad, cutting off his emotional feelings in order to get through the years until he could leave home.

'My son could have done with some reassuring words from me at that moment. I was fine with the practical stuff – meeting the headteacher keeping a diary of any incidents my son experienced, all that was fine – but showing that emotional side of me would mean bringing the hurt back I felt as a boy. I'm no good at that stuff, and I wasn't ready to face my past.' Steve was not alone in the effects of such discipline.

Austin: 'My brother and dad don't talk really; they are distant. My brother has not forgiven our dad for some of the beatings he gave us. It would be good if Dad would say sorry, but I can't see that happening because there is too much water under the bridge, but an apology from Dad may have gone some way in healing old wounds between them.'

Barriers to unresolved childhood issues

There is no doubt in my mind, having sought the views of so many fathers, that:

- Some fathers believe that a traditional form of punishment that includes severe chastisement will make their sons, in particular, ready for the injustices they will experience in society. I would add that some of these fathers have transferred their own experiences from childhood and the punishment they received as a child to their own children as it's all they know.

- The fathers who received severe chastisement as children and have unresolved issues with their fathers tend not to have close relationships with their fathers. In fact, the majority of these fathers have little to no adult contact with their fathers and their childhood chastisement was cited as one of the main reasons.

- Fathers who do enjoy a close relationship with their own fathers have either confronted and discussed the issue with their fathers or chose to privately forgive by rationalising what happened to them. Confronting their fathers seemed to have cleared the air, leading to a better understanding between the two. Austin is a good example, whereby he avoided his dad for a number of years until he found the courage to approach him, when Austin was able to tell his father how he felt, thereby repairing their tense relationship.

- The fathers who decided to privately forgive their own fathers rationalised their decisions by stating that, at times, they deserved to be punished, or they conceded that such punishment was 'the way' among African and Caribbean fathers at the time. Everyone they knew faced similar chastisement and was willing to share their stories. This made the fathers feel as if they were not alone, rather than maximise their feelings of hurt, as they were made to feel as if others understood what they had gone through.

- I would love for fathers – men – to realise there is no harm or shame in seeking professional help to work through childhood issues. In extreme cases, some fathers faced what can only be considered child abuse. I know this is hard to accept because some of the men to whom I have spoken do not want to be associated or labelled with this type of terminology. Whatever you want to call it, one thing is clear: what is there to lose by seeking help if you feel you are still harbouring feelings of bitterness, resentment, and for some, hate towards your father? I met some fathers who would not have the opportunities to confront their fathers as they have passed away. However, they still have the opportunity to confront their demons if they can find the courage to do so and seek counselling, and there are a number of organisations that provide support with childhood traumas.

Finding another way to discipline your children

From talking to fathers, it is clear that some fathers with childhood relationship issues with their own parents can, at times, struggle to cope and become upset or angry quickly with their children. This can push them beyond their limits because their parents did not show them parent-coping mechanisms as children. Steve wanted to learn new disciplinary strategies that he felt were more humane, and he hoped other fathers could advise him.

The answers from the group varied depending on their experience, but a common theme existed: the modern approach to disciplining your children should be age-appropriate to the misbehaviour. If your young child is stalling before going to bed or messing around whilst brushing his teeth before school, this may not be viewed as serious as not completing their homework, breaking curfew time to return home, or swearing. What I seem to hear from most fathers – and it's backed up by the Joseph Rowntree Foundation study by Barn and Rogers into parenting beliefs and practises – is that families saw disciplining their children to be mainly the father's responsibility.

Maybe some of the first generation's reluctance to subject their children to some of the beatings they endured has led to a decline in the use of the belt. Also, the public and authorities whose duty it is to protect children would not tolerate such chastising methods from the past being used in today's sensitive climate. However, 'disciplinarian' dads do bring up an interesting question: has the relaxation of discipline within the home and a more child-centred approach to parenting led to more wayward children and teenagers? We all hear stories of, on the one side of the continuum, rude and unruly teenagers who show a complete lack of respect towards adults and on the other side, the more extreme cases of knife and gun crime. I often hear adults saying, 'I blame the parents; these children have not been brought up properly.'

It is not so much that 'disciplinarian' parents may be too strict or 'reasoned' parents too soft. The fact is that the answer lies in both approaches. Disciplining your child should be a fluid concept that needs to be measured before a punishment is decided upon, and it must include both approaches to be effective. You might think this stance is sitting on the fence, as some fathers do, but the truth is there are times when you will need to be strict and times when you will need to be measured. Otherwise, you would have a situation whereby a father becomes one-dimensional in his approach to punishing his children. This can lead to a child being either physically abused with all the psychological effects it brings or where a child becomes boundary-less and difficult to control.

Neither scenario is good for the child or the parents, so to decide which approach is better at any given time is first to identify how serious your child's misbehaviour is and whether your child has previously been warned, and then thinking about the level of appropriate punishment or 'sanction'. Trying to avoid reverting to the old response of physical chastisements – such as the belt, slipper, tree branch, or anything else at hand – can prove difficult for some. It is the power of our words that should matter followed by the sanction and not the other way around. If we really want our children to learn what they did is wrong, we need to communicate this to them because, as I remember, a beating just made you scared to do it again, but there was no learning. Getting the balance right is the key, as is bringing up balanced individuals who not only understand the difference between right and wrong but also the need for parents to exercise sanctions against them when needed.

What was interesting is that young dads said that using the belt on their children has never been an issue; they just do not do it. Interestingly, some of their fathers did hit them, but it was mainly with their hands and around their legs or bottoms rather than with a belt or other objects at hand. So, a transformation of approaches to punishment has taken place and filtered down to the next generation. For some, their hands have replaced the belt as the chosen tool of punishment. A younger dad recalls his second-generation father disciplining him:

> **Mark:** 'I swear my dad didn't know his own strength. My dad's hands were hard. I can still feel the stinging sensation on the back of my legs as I speak to you now.'

These young fathers' children, on the whole, seemed to have been spared what the second-generation fathers had to endure in the 1960s and 1970s from their fathers. In the 1990s, a combination of the rights of children were enshrined in the Children Act, 1989, and Children's rights groups, such as the NSPCC, were effective in encouraging even hardened, disciplinarian parents to look at new approaches to disciplining their children. Therefore, a softer approach to discipline was encouraged in certain cultural groups. The rise in child-centred parenting meant that parents – fathers in particular – are spending much more time with their children than their dads before them. The rise in work-life balance has meant that fathers are more able to participate in leisure activities, take paternity leave, and become more involved in the school run, going to the park, and the very popular birthday parties. Maybe a modern-day attachment to leisure and new laws and an understanding of the chastisement of children has led to fathers' desiring alternative ways to discipline their children.

The use of 'sanctions'

It would seem that although the physical punishment of children still prevails within some cultures, there is, thankfully, a decline in the use of the belt. That is not to say that children are not receiving physical punishment, but we hope that parents are thinking about a range of 'sanctions', rather than limiting themselves to a prescriptive path like our fathers did. Hopefully, the belt is a dying method of discipline because it is a cruel and outdated method and can legally land parents in court on the grounds of physical abuse. This message seems to be getting through to most disciplinarian fathers.

Father: 'Listen (sensing the tide had turned against the tried and tested chastising methods he had learned from his dad): I'm not saying the belt is always the only way, but it's the only way I know. That's how my dad brought me up, and look – I turned out okay.'

This was his way of conceding that fathers' 'disciplinarian' methods may not be the best way forward in this day and age.

As a group of men, we did not expect him to confess his history of disciplining his children. We accepted and appreciated his honest contribution and know that, as a male, it is not always easy to concede that your way is not always the right way.

Most groups I met understood the concept of appropriate or 'reasoned' discipline. The question really is how do we deal with and decide what 'sanctions' are reasonable and measured in a given situation? What level of 'sanctions' should be given to our children when, for instance, they miss curfew time, backchat an adult, do not complete their chores, wake up late for school/college, start a fight, and so on?

Each group with which I met and discussed the topic were so keen to share their experiences, give advice, and try to find answers for one another. It does not often happen that, as men, we can share our ideas and not feel as if we should always have the answers because, frankly, we did not. That was our time to lay everything on the table and learn from one another. Most groups or individual fathers with whom I spoke were happy to grab the opportunity with both hands! So excited at our newfound freedom to test out their uncertainties without feeling judged, we attempted to grade children's misbehaviours and sanctions. After a while, we realised that agreeing on the severity of a child's behaviour and associated 'sanction' proved a lot harder than expected. Have a look at the chart we drew up to see what you think:

Sanction grading table

Misbehaviour	Grade	Sanction
Stealing money/ other criminal offences	4+	Dependent on age, loss of all privileges and some external sanctions could include the Police/courts/damaged reputation within the family
Not completing chores	2	No chores, no fun-time
Not completing homework on time	2	**No consensus** – Dependent on age
Chatting back (rude) to parents/ adults	3	**No consensus**, but viewed as serious enough – limit access to PlayStation /Wii/social media/going to mall damage to families' reputation externally
Lying to parents	3	Dependant on how big lie is – loss of privileges – you decide
Fighting	2	**No consensus** – who started the fight?
Poor grades at school/college/ university	3	If child struggling, homework support needed and encouragement rather than a sanction. But if due to a lack of discipline to study, parents to take more responsibility in monitoring
Struggles to get up in morning	1	Work on by trying different strategies rather than starting with sanctions – going to bed earlier
Drunk	2	Morning hangover may be punishment enough!
Hard drug taking: crack, cocaine	4+	Professional support needed, loss of allowance to stop financing habit

Poor behaviour at school/college/ university	3	No friends over and time out alone seeing s/he cannot behave around people, loss of allowance
Soft drug taking: cannabis/weed	2	**No consensus** – scare them (depending on age) with drugs video and talk before hard drugs use sets in!
Playing too much computer games/ social media	1	Limit activity to time agreement
Breaking curfew	3	If treating them like an adult is not working, treat like a child – they hate it!

Key

1. Less significant
2. Significant

3. Serious
4. Extremely serious

As the chart shows, it is hard to gain consensus on all misbehaviours and agree on the appropriate 'sanction.' Also, the graph does not show mitigating circumstances that we discussed, so some sanctions, such as soft drugs or fighting, may seem out of context. I found that fathers had differing values, so the severity of the 'sanction' would also vary, but the important thing is that we discussed the type of scenarios parents have to deal with day in day out with their children and teenagers, and we do not give mixed messages to our children that one day, a certain behaviour is okay and the next day it is not. That just leads to our children becoming confused. What we are clear about is that if you are thinking about how to 'sanction' your child or teenager, you are thinking about his long-term well-being and your role as a boundary setter. In other words, what is acceptable behaviour and what is not. Rather than make impulsive decisions around sanctions, we are trying to make thoughtful and consistent decisions to ensure the 'sanctions' fit the presenting behaviour and our children know exactly where they stand with us, the parents.

Fathers understand that this modern-day method of thinking before acting is better than an old-fashioned 'box around the head' without so much as an explanation or warning for such actions. For those 'disciplinarian' fathers, we have to accept that we have a difference of opinions, and there are avenues they can use from the chart to decide on the severity of the 'sanction' they want to use. It also means that we are trying to be consistent with our 'sanction' decision making. If we are clear and consistent at an early age with our children, they will be clear about their boundaries and what we expect of them.

Goodbye to the belt – finding a new approach to discipline

It is clear to me that having later spoken to grandfathers in the chapter **Back to the Future – Grandfathers Speak**, there was a general acknowledgement that using a belt to chastise children is outdated and something they regret doing, but these grandfathers found it difficult to discuss with me and their peers. After all, the world has changed since they were young fathers, and they have somewhat mellowed in old age. To see the change whilst their grandchildren got away murder while their parents could not, was a fact not lost on the few 'disciplinarian' fathers I met, who tried in vain to argue their case for the continuation of using the belt. So, let's put the belt where it belongs in the bin or around your waist and turn to some more positive approaches to disciplining our children. Try some of the ideas from the above 'sanction' chart with your children or teenagers when the time arises. Make a mental picture of the chart to guide you to the desired action. See what happens (how do you feel and how do your children react) whilst you give out the 'sanction' and share your experience with your friends and family.

Here is a light-hearted story to emphasise the fact that thinking about which 'sanction' to use can be very effective.

One father explained that his eight-year-old son ran into the girls' toilets at school several times, and each time the teacher spoke to him, it was obvious that he thought his actions were funny. Now, let us not forget that this boy is only eight years old and has a lot to learn about socially acceptable behaviour. The parents spoke to their son and explained why he should not enter the girls' toilets. The group agreed that the activity of running into the girls' toilets at his age was a low grade – less significant (1) – compared to other types of misbehaviour, but his action is socially unacceptable, and his response to a ticking off from his teacher meant the grading had been raised to significant enough (2). There was a possibility of his continuing to run into the toilet and obtaining a sanction mark (on his behaviour card at school). Everything seemed okay for a few weeks until the teacher spoke to his mother to inform her there was a further incident. The father was furious with his son. 'I wanted to hit him when I saw him after work because he knows how to behave, but I had calmed down a little but still shouted at him.' The alpha male's attitude of 'If you can't hear, you must feel' was strong in this father and usually produces an instantaneous response, but this approach is only for a short space of time. A new approach was needed, and his wife suggested that rather than just shout at him, they should withhold privileges he enjoys doing.

The parents spoke to their son and explained that they were disappointed with him, and they would decide on his 'sanction'. The boy was used to instant punishment from his dad, but this was new, something the boy was not used to, and the wait for his 'sanction' was killing him.

The next day, his parents announced that their son would not be allowed to ride his bike all weekend, and it was expected that he would not repeat running into the girls' toilets at school again, otherwise, the 'sanction' would be repeated the following weekend. Needless to say, their son never entered the girls' toilets again because he loves riding his bike, and he linked his action to the loss of something he enjoys doing. The outcome for the parents using this new approach was that they felt in control because they communicated with each other and had the sanction chart to call upon for guidance. The father felt that he was more in tune with his emotions and was able to see the situation for what it was rather than out of frustration, and most importantly, their son had learned a valuable lesson, that his bike was a privilege he could continue to earn to ride or lose the privilege to ride and respect for separate toilets.

How would you have handled the situation? What do you think was the pivotal point in his parents' decision making? Did the 'sanction' fit the presenting behaviour?

The father explained that his old method of a quick shout and telling his son off was not really dealing with his sons' behaviour or having the desired effect. On reflection, he realised his son did not have to think about the consequences of his behaviour, and he chose expedient methods of punishment (a quick shout or a slap on the leg), rather than dealing with the issue at hand.

Life is so hectic and fast-moving that his punishment mirrored his life. He needed to put more thought into it and be more creative to allow himself a little more time to reflect on what to do. The 'sanction' system we have spoken about, and his wife's timely intervention made him think about how to deal with his son's running into the girls' toilet. Some of the fathers have started to apply the 'sanction' grading system in their families with various adaptations to the basic table we drew up, and the results have been promising. We suggest you speak to your friends and use the 'sanction' list grading to find out their views.

The table can really open your eyes, lead to discussion and even disagreement within your circle of friends as to how to grade certain types of behaviour. Just like some of the fathers could not come to a consensus, you may find the same amongst your friends. As fathers, you know your children, what makes them tick, their likes and dislikes, moods, time for encouragement and confidence building, and time for 'sanctions', so it's your decision on the most appropriate grading followed by the appropriate 'sanction' for your children. In fact, you don't even have to use our crude table; you may just prefer to be aware of how you choose to 'sanction' your children in the future. Either way, you are being a thoughtful and effective parent in doing so, and you are likely to feel less guilty as your decisions will be measured and reasonable.

The majority of the fathers' messages are clear. For those parents who are still using the belt, let's throw it away and vow to find new and more effective ways to discipline our children. But a word of caution: I am not saying that you have to change everything and follow the table guide rigidly. The fatherhood groups have devised a basic table as a guide out of thoughtful love for their children and the desire not to be remembered, like some of our fathers, as belt-wielding disciplinarians. If you are a father who still uses the belt or other objects to discipline your child and have decided to take on some of the fathers' ideas, it means you are preparing yourself for positive change, and I promise that you will feel better for it. This means that you are no longer allowing your frustration to dictate how you deal with the challenges your children are bound to throw your way once in a while. This is your chance to break free from your father's generation and start afresh with new approaches.

The fact is that, sometimes, it's not our children's behaviour that is the problem but the fact that we are so wound up and stressed due to work and life in general. It is more about how we deal with our stresses and their behaviour that counts because, at the same time, we are showing them how we deal with stressful situations. When your children are older and wiser, they will understand that your decisions were due to your unconditional love for them and your quest to find better and less guilt-ridden discipline methods to teach them right from wrong. You never know – they may use your creative methods to 'sanction' their future children, your grandchildren!

Healing the past with our fathers

This sensitive topic is also dealt with extensively in the chapter **Back to the Future – Grandfathers Speak**, looking at our fathers' evolutions in Africa and the Caribbean, where their disciplined approaches were moulded. I could not, however, end this chapter without mentioning the present-day impact that being hit with the belt during childhood has had on some fathers. The belt beating as children and our fathers' emotional detachment from us as young boys is mentioned in the chapter on **masculinity; helping your son grow up the right way** has affected some of us more than others in adulthood. A lot of these fathers have carried their childhood experiences into adulthood and are still hurting inside because there has been no avenue for closure with their fathers. A reluctance to open old wounds seems to be the motivating factor for their silence. They have been unable to seek emotional resolution, either within themselves or their fathers or through professional help. The emotional scars from the discipline they endured has, at times, rendered them unable to have as close a relationship with their own children as they would wish.

> **Steve:** 'My brother would benefit from talking to our dad about the beating he got, but it's not going to happen because our dad is not approachable in that way... I wish one of them would talk because there is a distance between them that won't be mended unless one of them makes a move.'

I have spoken to some fathers like Austin, who admitted talking to their dads about how they felt about their past discipline and how they felt an acute injustice had happened to them. It has helped their healing process to express their feelings and show their dads that they have grown up and are no longer scared of them. Although, in general, the relationship was one of respect, a lot of second-generation fathers admitted to fearing what their fathers would do to them if they messed up.

Rather than have a father-son talk about the consequences of our actions, their way was to provide us with swift punishment. As mentioned before, such experiences have had different effects on fathers' parenting. Some have struggled to openly say I love you or praise their children or partners for their achievements. These fathers say they really want to feel raw emotion for their children, but deep down, something is stopping them from doing so. To show such open and unconditional love would mean opening the child within them, who received little love from their fathers or families. Some are absent from the family home primarily due to attachment and commitment issues, while others are afflicted by their inner demons. There seems to be a pattern, a personality trait: they tend to run away (mentally and emotionally) when it comes to real affection giving and long-term commitment in the family environment. How do you show an emotion such as love to your children and partner when you never received it from your father or family? Other fathers have embraced their past and resolved their negative past experiences to ensure they nurture their immediate families, stick together, meet regularly, and give their time and attention to their children and wives.

> **Father:** 'I wanted to give to my family the love and connection I never received from my father. I am close to my son and made a conscious effort to give him hugs rather than the only physical contact we have is when I punish him. I have friends who have affection issues because of how they were treated as kids, so I wanted to break that cycle in my family.'

This is why, as fathers, we have continued to spread the message of the importance of getting to know, talk, and play with our sons and daughters because if we do not take an interest in our children now, when will we ever find the time to do so? On a positive note, the older fathers – who are now grandfathers – who used the belt with such unflinching accuracy have acknowledged that times have moved on when it comes to discipline. Their way to discipline was the only way they knew back then, and present fathers are now using new methods to discipline their children.

It is not too late for any grandfathers reading this book to explain to their grown sons why they used the belt, and in some cases, apologise. Only you will know whether your punishment has placed a wedge between you and your adult son. Of course, not all grandfathers overdid the discipline, but if you feel you might have done so, it's never too late to talk – your son awaits you.

A Safe Haven: the Importance
of Our Extended Families

'You don't choose your family. They are God's gift to you as you are to them.'
– Desmond Tutu

Two boys from a rival school were looking for me. My crime? Well, I dared to suggest their students were dumb for coming to our school to pick fights rather than study. My comments were not considered a proper 'diss' in anyone's language, but tensions between the schools were high, so one day after school, they came looking for the boy who had made the comments to teach me a lesson – hell, to beat me up! Now, this was before the days of Mike Tyson, but one of those boys had Tyson's menacing build, which meant that no one messed with him if they knew what was good for their health. With his image in my head, I wasn't about to wait around the school to be pounded into the ground – I loved life too much to allow that to happen – so, self-preservation and avoiding, a.k.a. Mike Tyson was high on my agenda that day.

I took refuge at one of my auntie's houses – she lived near the school – and I stayed there until the commotion had died down, and it was safe to walk the streets again. My aunt and uncle always made me feel welcome by feeding me and talking about all kinds of things. I was allowed to sit in the front room, which was usually locked and only for adults. I swear that's where I discovered my love of food. The more I ate, the more food that would appear on my plate. By the time I had left my aunt's house and walked home, I was so full and content, I had forgotten about the Mike Tyson threat. My aunt's home, along with a few other family homes scattered around East London, was my safe haven. It gave me a choice of being on the streets or in the safety of their homes. The extended family has provided a foundation and safety net for families around the world for centuries. I remember my mother feeding relatives who had fallen on hard times, and I am sure those families, in turn, had helped us in times of need. What these generations lacked in money, they made up for in kindness.

Fond memories of our extended family

Not only did I visit my cousins when I needed to hide from someone or something, but they were also a part of my usual house rounds. I enjoyed playing with my cousins or impressing them with a new girlfriend. I knew my way around those houses, I was treated as if I were special, and the treatment was reciprocal when they visited our home.

Of course, there were the odd chores I sometimes had to perform, but I did these willingly as I got back much more than I had to put in. This was my extended family, and it provided me with a safe haven throughout my childhood. I did not always have to seek out my parents for assistance – I could rely on my aunts and uncles for any number of things. I was as welcome as a son in their homes, and the door was always open for me and my brothers and sisters.

Cousins and friends sometimes joined us for dinner and were treated as a part of the immediate family. In fact, if they wanted to stay the night, no fuss was made; an extra pillow was found, and although our beds were more squashed with an extra body in it, no one cared. To this day, I do not understand how the bed did not collapse with all the weight. Some people say the workmanship on furniture in the past was built to last compared to today.

The role of the extended family was pivotal, holding large families together and absorbing all the punches that life threw at us. Whether siblings got on or not, Sunday in my household was special, and my memories will be everlasting. These meals were a great way to come together and heal rifts between family members, whether they still lived at home or not. I remember when I was not getting on with one of my sisters, but as we bit into our mother's fried chicken, we both just smiled at each other. Good food and a family gathering had a way of healing even the nastiest of arguments.

A perfect example of this can be seen in the classic American film, 'Soul Food,' staring Nia Long. If you have not seen this film, I strongly suggest that you do. It shows how even during adversity and personality differences, families can still come together when needed. The extended families' contribution to holding the fabric of the family together cannot be underestimated. My parents, aunts, and uncles made the importance of sticking together no matter what clear to me from an early age.

This message was also passed on to the fathers with whom I discussed this topic. The majority of them remembered being told many times by different adults in their families. Eventually, when we had all left home, visiting my parents, aunts, and uncles brought me great comfort and fond memories. I was older and could appreciate their company and life stories more than I did as a boy, and of course, the fish cakes and fried chicken tasted just as good. I still felt a sense of belonging within the homes of my extended family long after I had left home. We did not have much compared to some children, but we had each other. It is difficult to explain our sense of freedom and adventure to today's children because our extended family lived within walking distance of where we lived. However, this close proximity to our extended family has changed so drastically over the years.

A few older fathers spoke of fond memories of visiting their extended families. One father remembered his aunts and uncles giving him extra pocket money. He often watched cricket with his uncles in the days when the West Indies cricket team was a force to be reckoned with. The excitement, the banter, and the laughter during cricket were special times for him. So many fathers remembered being in the company of their cousins during informal house gatherings and more formal events, such as christenings and weddings. Friday night dominos seemed to have been a popular pastime in homes during the 70s and 80's. Some fathers enjoyed listening to the ribbing during the domino games, listening to music, and the centrality of food at such gatherings. They would stay late at cousins' homes during the weekend until the message to get their backsides home had reached them.

Modern day fears: The creation of 'cotton wool' children

The opportunities for children to venture out and explore the neighbourhood were much more open to children like me 40 years ago compared to nowadays. Funny – we are one of the generations that was able to enjoy its freedom who are now the very parents that limit their children venturing out to play in their neighbourhoods. This has led to the term 'cotton wool' children, and child professionals from various fields blame parents for overprotecting their children by not letting them out of their homes to play and allowing too much home entertainment, leading to a lack of exercise, bad diets, and in some cases, obesity. But the biggest criticism targeted at parents and establishments – such as schools and organised sports teams – is not allowing our children to learn or be exposed to some of life's setbacks such as losing, getting a disappointing score on a test, or not allowing a child to come in last during an activity. They are not allowed to make judgement calls that could mean they fall over and possibly hurt themselves, nor are age-appropriate children allowed to walk unaccompanied to local shops.

As fathers, we spoke about the changes we have seen whilst growing up in Britain that may account for our change in attitude towards our children's safety.

- Changing communities have meant we no longer know or trust our neighbours. In a recent survey, fewer than half of the respondents were able to name five neighbours residing on their road. In times gone by, you got to know your neighbours' families who would live in the same houses for generations. However, due to the transient nature of people due mainly to employment and the rise in short-term lettings, some long-standing communities have lost cohesiveness and trust, preventing their children from playing freely in their communities.

- Changing communities have led to families becoming more private about their lives. We no longer have open-door attitudes where our neighbours are concerned because we do not know them well enough. Yes, polite greetings occur, but how many of us actually pop next door for a drink and a chat? So, our children are not playing in our homes and those of their immediate neighbours, so we are unlikely to let them play outside.

- Parents fear – and at times, irrationally perceive – that a paedophile might lurk on their streets or in the local parks. I have heard parents stating that the McCann family's dreadful experience has reconfirmed to them that even on holidays, our children need protecting from strangers. This applies even more to our local streets, where the perception seems to be that strangers are just waiting for opportunities to pounce.

- The huge increase in cars using residential streets as 'rat runs' makes parents fearful of fatal car accidents. Also, we drive and chaperone our children to their weekend events – such as sports, parties, and school – so some children do not learn about street safety.

- 24-hour news means that we are exposed to national news rather than just local news. This can influence our views of the wider world, making us believe the dangers to our families have increased over the years. There is a lot of debate about whether, statistically, our children are in any more danger than we were 40 years ago, or whether, as parents we are just exposed to more information from TV and the Internet.

- Maybe we are much more aware of the dangers that can befall children in neighbourhoods than our parents were. Remember that some of them never played as children in Britain, having come as adults, and they may be unable to see or experience some of the dangers we did. Maybe we are just wiser than our parents when it comes to the dangers lurking in the streets.

- The fourfold increase in health and safety legislation assessments of risk throughout our lives means that we have become much more aware of dangers that exist and look for ways to minimise potential dangers, especially in relation to our children. This is good to a point, but we have become so conditioned to look for danger that we can disable our children when it comes to making their own judgement calls in relation to risk whilst playing, climbing, or crossing the road.

The effect of our exposure to 24-hour mainly negative news from around the world, the abduction of children, the never-ending world disasters and general street muggings have led to a psychological battening down the hatches. The consequence is that our children are kept in the safety of our four walls where we can see them. This decision means that our children spend a lot more time in their bedrooms being entertained by computer games and social media. When our children complain they are bored, we get angry and state that they have so many toys compared to when we were their age.

Some fathers felt that our children get bored too easily and lack the ability to use their imaginations to find sustainable play within the home. What we have forgotten is that when we were growing up, we had many options. We could play all day in our homes, play with our neighbours in their homes, on the streets, or in the park. All of these activities were done without our parents' supervision to watch over our safety. It is true to say that our parents came from countries where children were allowed to wander outside the home within the community, where everyone and all generations knew each other.

The new phenomenon of 'cotton wool' culture as an approach by parents can lead to children lacking coping skills. Sandy MacLean of the Scottish Further Education Unit looked at the mental health of the UK's 16- to 24-year-olds. MacLean stated that in order for young people to develop resilience, they must experience adversity, but they are increasingly protected from hard knocks by their parents. She goes on to make a general point about the state of affairs: 'Young people are not fragile; they can be likened to springs or balls. People can bounce back psychologically after being knocked out of shape, just like nature.' There are so many examples of the cushioning of our children when they face disappointment. For example, at some schools, the policy is to have non-competitive sports days. The schools are concerned because some children react badly to losing.

Most fathers disagreed with their schools' attitudes towards competition, believing that schools should be creative and have a mixture of team and individual competition without the focus on an individual winner. Competition is a part of life whether we like it or not, and children should be exposed to age-appropriate competition and not hidden from disappointment. One African Caribbean father who found support from some quarters was adamant that such cushioning of children would not allow them to be tough enough to survive in the real world.

> **Father:** 'Listen, if you guys want to cushion your children from all the bumps in life, go ahead, but you are making them soft. Some people sitting here today because of the colour of their skin will have faced discrimination at work, in the streets, wherever, so I have to prepare my kids to be tough because life is not fair, and they must learn to be strong and stand tall because they will need to scrap with people who don't like them because of the colour of their skin.'

Of course, the actual attitudes and practices in the home varies amongst the fathers. The less anxious fathers have taken more relaxed attitudes towards allowing their children to venture out to local shops or walk to their friends'. Their decisions are based on the maturity of their children, the distance, and the number of roads that need to be crossed. These fathers tend to discuss with their wives the types of activities and risks involved before the events to allow them the chance to make informed decisions. Invariably, practical and staggered approaches are used when allowing their children partial freedom to show their responsibility. Other more anxious fathers admitted that, along with their partners, they had not reached the stage where they felt comfortable allowing their children to venture out with friends or go to local shops unaccompanied. They admitted to probably listening to the news too much, and the negative information gained seemed to render them unsure whether to allow their children a bit of freedom.

One dad spoke about his ten-year-old daughter going to a local shop as he watched her cross the zebra crossing. However, he was filled with so much anxiety he ended up accompanying her to the shop.

What I found is that when and how you allow your child to start taking those little steps is subjective. Families of the same culture have different views about when they think their children are ready to walk to local shops, take a bus to school, go to the cinema, party with their friends, or have a sleepover at a friend's house. One father's sentiments seem to represent so many views I have heard:

> **Father:** 'We understand that the world we grew up in has changed so much. My teenage daughter can go out, but she needs to continue to act mature otherwise, this could change. We constantly argue about how far is considered safe when she wants to travel to a friend's home. I am protective, but the dangers are great compared to when I was growing up.'

So, parents are clearly split on this topic, from the parents who feel we are too protective towards our children to those who are struggling to let go. In general, parents feel they need to continue to be vigilant and make judgements that will allow their children more freedom or experience disappointments in life. Some fathers positively disagreed with the analysis of cotton wool children and advocated for parents to allow their children to take more controlled risks or be exposed to disappointments. They argue that parents throughout history have always been protective towards their young, and whether through custom or tradition, make decisions around their children's age-appropriate activities. These differences of opinion amongst the fathers show that a healthy debate is taking place, and new ideas are shared that provide us all with food for thought.

The decline of our extended families

The experience of fathers growing up was the importance of sticking together through thick and thin, so what has happened? The extended family was our way of life, and although they still exist in pockets, the actual interaction and interdependency between family members seem to be on the decline in our communities.

I believe that the decline of the extended family is to our personal and family's detriment. My extended family protected me from so much potential danger, and at times, stopped me from being on the streets when gang-fighting or National Front activity threatened to spill over. Being near one of my cousins' houses meant that I could keep from being sucked into activities I did not want to do, or of which my parents would not approve. I do not believe teenagers have the same extended families that we came to value as safe havens for so many reasons. The feeling of belonging in so many different homes meant I felt protected. Invariably, my fear of what was happening on the street, such as being targeted by the then National Front, were sometimes dispelled if I was physically near a cousin's home.

What if I did not have these safe havens to go to when I was a teenager? I hate to think about what might have happened, but I feel that you can see the lack of family safe havens for the young and the consequences it can entail.

There are many reasons for the decline in the extended family, which I will go on to talk about in a while. The question for fathers is if we still value having extended families, or have they already outlived their usefulness in modern-day Britain? Our parents formed a part of the so-called first generation of Africans and Caribbeans and many other countries from the Commonwealth, such as India and Pakistan, who settled in Britain throughout the 1960s and 1970s. Our parents recreated the extended family model from their homelands, exporting the model to Britain. Whether this was a conscious decision, this family type endured and survived the cold winter climates and fog of 1950s and 1960s Britain.

These families were interdependent on each other for childcare, social events, community money-saving systems known as 'Pardners', DIY, car maintenance, advice, guidance, and so on. Safety in numbers was important in a sometimes hostile and alien country, and it is a system being recreated time and time again by the latest batch of newly arrived immigrants. The generations of aunts, uncles, and grandparents who allowed my siblings and me a safe and loving place to hang and play have either passed away or migrated back home. This has left a huge void for second-generation adults like myself today. The foundations of these families were the mothers and aunties who ensured that the bonds between cousins stayed strong by their interpersonal communication skills, get-togethers, and warmth towards adults and children alike. Unfortunately, once this changed, for a while the second generation continued but did not seem able or willing to continue these traditions, and slowly, the model and togetherness became splintered and no longer the norm within most families. Some fathers in the groups I met have been able to continue their extended

49

family support model through effort and developing strong relationship bonds. But I have also met a lot of fathers who admit that the decline of their extended families' regular contact can be traced back to their mother and grandmother's absence. There is no doubt in my mind that the senior females bonded families together, and once this strong figure had gone, there was not always a replacement to continue the role. This decline has had a direct effect on whether our children are able to identify with their extended families, getting to see and play with their cousins like we use to, and watching out for each other.

Black Flight – Life in the suburbs

This is a term first coined to explain white working-class families 'made good' in the 1970s and '80s, moving out of inner-city areas to the suburbs of Essex. These families were seen as socially mobile, having gained some qualifications and promotions at work, enabling them to secure better work security and income compared to their parents. These families could financially afford to move out of the areas in which their families had lived for generations, thus improving their children's schools and general quality of life by having bigger houses and gardens and less crime.

A similar phenomenon took place to a lot of Black families in the late 20th century. Their educational attainment led to better and higher paid jobs compared to their parents. Their aspiration was to have a better standard of living, and this was realised through hard work and promotions. The Thatcher years' propaganda of investment in brick and mortar and the deregulation of financial services meant that larger mortgages were a reality for more families.

As second-generation children, we took the opportunity with both hands. Some followed white working-class families out of the immediate inner-city and strategically placed ourselves on the edges of the two. Whether you are from North, South, East, or West London, Luton,

Birmingham, Leeds, Manchester, Liverpool, or Derby, the trend is similar. All towns and cities have areas to which people aspire to move to once they have made a bit of money. Some fathers were aware of their decision about just how far to move from their immediate families. The areas into which they moved had few Asian and Black families. If they had moved farther out, there was likely to have been less of a racial mix, and this was considered unacceptable or dangerous as they might experience hostility in predominately white neighbourhoods.

So, a middle ground was struck whereby the short distance from their families' roots enabled them to keep in regular contact with family, without compromising the bigger house and garden of which they dreamed. Other fathers talked about their reservation about moving too far into the suburbs as older family members struggled to travel to see them as public transportation links were poor. As one father stated, "I would love my auntie to visit me more, just like I used to visit her when I was a boy. I used to walk to her house, but there is no way she could walk to see me. I live much too far now. Unless her daughter or I go and drive her up, I don't see her much. That is a real shame."

I applaud families who strive to improve themselves socially, professionally, and economically, as we all know this is not easy to achieve. It takes years of sacrifice to climb the ladder of promotion at work, to save and build a financial portfolio, and eventually buy the dream house you've always wanted for your children to play in a big garden you never had. I understand as I have been there. I even went to the extent of ensuring that I had a spare bedroom for my nieces and nephews to stay in. The fact of the matter is that they do come to stay, but not as often as I had hoped, due to poor transportation links that made popping round difficult for them. I would love for them to be able to pop round like I was able to go to my cousins' homes as a young boy, but my neighbourhood is no longer their neighbourhood. I feel like I have let them down and taken away their freedom to come to see me without needing their parents to accompany them. I sometimes wonder at the personal cost our move to the suburbs had on maintaining our extended families' way of life.

This Black flight has led to some families unintentionally isolating other extended family members from freely visiting them. I say 'unintentionally' because what I discovered was that people followed their aspirations to do better rather than try to escape from their families. Also, we were encouraged to believe in the importance of the much-trumpeted nuclear family. These families were seen as the ideal family model due to their self-reliance. A few fathers admitted to not getting on with their in-laws, so moving out to put distance between them, seemed attractive.

However, the majority of families moving to the suburbs assumed that their families would just come to visit, and little thought was given to public transportation links for the old and young who do not drive and depend on the buses and Tube to get around. So, the very people who benefit from the extended family (the young) and the people who would assist in its upkeep (the old) are at a disadvantage.

The extended family – role in childcare

Look no further than the change from the informal care of our children within the extended family to the formal nursery setting in the last 20 years. Prior to the change to formal childcare, most families dropped their children off at their mothers, grandparents, great aunts, or close friends' homes before setting off for work safe in the knowledge that their family loves their children as much as they do.

The decline of elders in our extended families, the rise in women entering the workplace, and the physical move away from communities and the interdependency of others means that alternative and more convenient childcare has to be sought. It's difficult to ask Cousin to babysit now that he or she is 20 years old, and you haven't seen them since they were children.

Also, young grandparents who would have traditionally stayed at home are now working to make ends meet and are not available on a regular basis during the day. I know that my brothers and sisters benefited from the time my parents were in Britain to look after their children before they returned to Dominica, but by the time I'd had children, this option was no longer open to us as most of my close extended family had also returned.

As the fatherhood groups discussed the changes, we realised that changes in childcare arrangements were out of necessity rather than choice when they actually thought about who they really wanted to look after their flesh and blood. Having to seek other childcare arrangements was difficult, so without the security and love their families would give whilst caring for their children, it was replaced with the search for regulated, accountable, reputable nurseries for the care of their children.

But this came at a financial cost, hence the rise of private nurseries. Nowadays, a lot of working families depend on specialised private childcare organisations for their under five-year-old children. I have friends, family, and work colleagues who use the varying types of care provisions available to them, as did we when our children were younger. From day nurseries and childminders to after school clubs for over fives, all of these provisions have a few things in common, namely that your children are most likely looked after by non-family members, and you will pay them weekly or monthly for their service. Most of the fathers and their partners are resigned to using nurseries at some time in their children's infancies as a way to ensure women are able to pursue their careers, as the bulk of childcare still seems to fall on the women. The fathers admitted an initial anxiety on both sides with such a formal arrangement outside of their families. Fathers spoke about their wives feeling guilty having to leave their children with non-family members, but the reality of today's economic climate is that two-income families have become a necessity. It seems that having to hand over the trust of our children to a non-family member proved very difficult for the majority of families.

> **Father:** 'All parents seem to be doing the same, so you give it a go, hoping things will work out. As much as you want to, you can never quite trust a stranger with your child like you could your own blood.'

Some fathers remembered their parents going to work and leaving the eldest child in charge until one of the parents got home, or an upstairs neighbour kept an eye out on them. Of course, this type of arrangement may not be acceptable in Britain today, depending on the age of the eldest child, but there are many places in the world where this is still practised, and age is not a major issue.

Fathers spoke of finding a 'connection' with some staff that seems to understand and have a 'soft spot' for their children. Having workers that understand their feelings and standard of care made parents feel more comfortable about leaving their children for the day. The one disadvantage was that when the worker left, parents' stress levels tended to rise again. A few fathers spoke about the drop in standards at some nurseries as they expanded to increase their intake, losing the essence of providing a personal touch.

These smaller nurseries allowed for strong relationships with parents and particular workers who looked after their young, and they were willing to continue at the nursery. However, some fathers spoke about 'good workers' leaving and parents not wanting their children to stay at the nurseries. This placed a lot of pressure on parents who had to take time off from work to find alternative quality childcare and to help their children settle into new nurseries. These seem to be the two reasons why parents changing nurseries: They need to have a sense of the standards of care and that the workers actually care about their children.

The financial and emotional pressure on families in relation to childcare nowadays is huge compared to the extended family set-up of the past, which was much more cost-effective. The fathers unanimously thought the private nursery fee of around £800-1,000 per month was unreasonable, but due to the limited alternative childcare available, they had little choice but to pay. Also, there is extra pressure on parents to be on time as a lot of nurseries now charge for being late. A few fathers shared their stories about how the nursery fee was like having another mortgage or rent to pay, and the fines made them take risks whilst driving to the nursery in order not to face a hefty late fine.

The extended family used to provide this type of care in an informal manner for a fraction of the price we pay today, and no late fees were incurred. My mother, aunt, sister, and at times my uncle looked after my younger brother, sisters, and me within extended family homes. I do not remember feeling anxious as a child when my mum left us with an aunt, as these homes were familiar territory to me. I checked with my mum to ensure my line of thinking was correct, as I was young at the time. My mum was unsure as to what I was asking. 'Did I feel anxious? About what – leaving all of you with Aunty Pat? Why would I feel anxious when she is family?' My mum's response towards family looking after us still prevails today. I can see the difference in leaving your child with family members rather than non-family professionals. Although you know the standard of care is likely to be sufficient, just how much do the workers really care about your child? This is an impossible question to answer and rightly or wrongly, one that many parents naturally ask in private. My mum knew deep down that, barring a freak accident, we would be safe with our aunty, who would move heaven and earth to ensure our safety.

I wanted to gauge whether the change from informal to formal childcare has led to increased anxiety among parents. A minority of fathers were able to use family members for childcare. All of these family members are childminders in the childcare profession with a formal setup in their homes. One father had his sister looking after his one-year-old son because she had been made redundant in her job. He said that the arrangement was private, and he paid her half of what he would pay a childminder. This arrangement was the exception rather than the norm. Also, he did not have the threat of being fined for being late, so he ensured he respected his sister by arriving at the agreed-upon time. Still, she was flexible – if he was running late from work, he did not have to worry about being fined.

The formalisation and professional development of childcare arrangements do have benefits for parents. You enter into a contract with an organisation registered to provide government guided childcare. There is a worker and management hierarchy with qualified, insured, and varying levels of experienced workers. The amount of fees you pay depends on the area in which you live and the type (play or Montessori) of nursery to which you decide to send your children. What we as fathers have been grappling with is whether knowing if all of this provides us with a reassurance that adequate care is being provided, and we also believe that family members are the best people to provide this, but we understand that childcare options today are limited. We have become so self-reliant that we have lost the family and community childcare knowledge and contacts that extended family members are known to provide good, quality childcare and how we access it. At the moment, all of our efforts go towards looking for formal outside agencies rather than within our families and local communities. Maybe a sense of Individualism has developed over the last 25 years, and a little collectivism is needed.

I am not suggesting that we all give up our ways of life and start living in a kibbutz-type community where interdependency is an important daily function and childcare is provided within such a community, or that we go romantically back in time to informal childcare or requiring mothers to give up work to stay at home to look after the children; that would be a backwards step in so many ways. After talking to fathers, what we suggest is some form of family or local collectivism within the community to ease our stress levels and reassure parents that people we know are looking after our children. Of course, this idea will not be to everyone's liking, as you may well be quite happy with your present arrangement. There are other options whereby parents assist each other through their friendship circles to juggle the nursery/school runs and afterschool care. However, these seem to be very small-scale personal arrangements that work effectively and long may they continue.

Another option could also be within family and community organisations. There are already local community groups involved in wraparound care, whereby a combination of formal and informal childcare exists side by side. I understand that this may be a hard task depending on your type of family, friends, and the spirit of the community in which you live. Also, most family members, including some grandparents, have to earn a living and are not available to provide childcare during the day.

When talking to a grandfathers' group, they felt their age was a contributing factor as to why they could not look after their grandchildren on a full-time basis. Although they felt saddened by this, they have found creative ways to assist their families, contributing to childcare fees to help ease the financial burden, by looking after their grandchildren a few days a week or collecting them from from nursery or school. Also, there is the common theme that grandparents really enjoy looking after their grandchildren. They fuss over their grandchildren in a way they did not over us, and boy, do these children get away with a lot compared to us. You might think to yourself that your sons are in trouble for breaking something only to be told that it's okay and that it was an accident. In days gone by, the belt would have come out for me! It would seem that in their old age, grandparents have mellowed somewhat.

Buying into the nuclear family myth

This is where our traditional, extended, supportive family model comes into conflict with the much-trumpeted nuclear family model. The 'ideal' nuclear family with a mum, dad, 2.2 children (a boy and a girl), and a dog is the family type Britain has encouraged since the end of the Second World War. Smaller families made economic sense, and the advancement of medicine meant a lower infant mortality rate, leading to families no longer needing to have a lot of children. The nuclear family throughout the twentieth century was shown as being superior to other family types. Check out programmes on TV, and you will be hard-pressed to find large family units.

Of course, there are classics and contemporary shows in which larger families are found on TV, such as the cult American show 'The Cosby Show', 'Little House on the Prairie' My Wife and Kids and 'The Waltons', but these families were shown as nostalgic of days gone by rather than the present-day norm. What you saw in these families was a clear sense that although they may not always get on, they come together as a family when adversity strikes. The nuclear family is so-called due to its advantage of being self-sufficient, self-reliant, and self-managing. You can also see a sense of separation from the extended family by the desire to move away and start to define their own families. As mentioned before, this can lead to the minimisation of the extended family's importance, both practically and physically, due to the distance moved. I have heard – and I am sure you have, too – people talking about families who have four or five children. Large families still exist in certain cultures, but even in UK based Caribbean and African cultures, people are genuinely surprised when they come across a large family. This is how much our psyche has led us to believe and practise that having 2.2 children is the 'ideal' nuclear family. Interestingly, most of the families I met had two to three children, and the third child tended to be a final attempt to fulfil their desire to have children of both sexes.

Of course, depending on your upbringing, the importance of regularly seeing family members may vary. I know of some fathers who are in mixed relationships in which their white partners do not meet up regularly with their families. Of course, this is a generalisation and not a true reflection of families. Some fathers spoke of conflict with either their parents or siblings who felt they did not value meeting up as much as they used to. Some of their family members have accused these fathers of losing the priority for the family unit as they became immersed in the British way of life. The tension is sometimes resolved by a little give and take, but some fathers have remained stubborn and consciously minimised contact with family, although they know it causes them and their families a great deal of hurt.

> **Father:** 'I know my family are vexed with me, especially my two sisters, but I'm tired of being told where I should be on a Sunday, visiting and eating with them. Yeah, I don't mind meeting up sometimes, but not every Sunday! They blame my girlfriend, saying she is influencing me, taking me away from the family, and that can lead to a lot of arguments.'

Of course, these girlfriends are not to blame. It is the father's responsibility if he wants to keep in touch with his family and ensure his children get to play with and know their cousins to continue the important family links. In contrast, I spoke with a father who is dating an Italian woman, and she positively encourages him to visit his family, and she often participates in family activities. This may be due to her Italian upbringing and attitude towards the family. Family get-togethers are viewed as all-important, and she is loved by his family for ensuring he takes such a commitment seriously.

My point is that the so-called 'ideal' nuclear family has had a negative and erosive effect on our extended family models, whereby we value independence rather than interdependency (although there are pockets of good support systems in existence) and private self-reliance rather than family and community support. We have lost sight of our extended families and community worth and strength. We have bought into the myth that the nuclear family is the best type of family to aspire to have and that we do not need anyone else to survive. This practice has led to the nuclear family becoming insular and private, hardly knowing our neighbours as we go about our daily business.

I remember the first small house I bought. The community spirit was wonderful. Neighbours spoke to each other and helped each other out in many ways, such as looking after their houses whilst on holiday, gardening (my Scottish neighbour landscaped my garden), and house repairs. Whereas in another house into which we moved, there was no community spirit apart from a quick greeting as you closed your front door for the night. We didn't like the area and moved swiftly out. So, the area into which you move and your attitude towards your neighbours does play a part in the type of support system you have. Many fathers spoke about difficulties within their families (illness, relationship difficulties, financial problems, and childcare difficulties), and having to branch out to their extended families for assistance. Whether they were initially given a hard time from their families depended on their perception of whether they were still close or not.

Our English ways

Just a bit of humour: have you noticed how English in our ways we have become – fish and chips on a Friday night, queuing up and the reaction to a queue-jumper, moaning about the weather or just moaning in general, the love of tea/coffee, going to the pub, an obsession with football, and when someone knocks on your door, you think, 'Who is that? We haven't invited anyone to our home?' Some of our mindsets towards family and close friends visiting seems to be influenced by our feelings of the extent to which we are being inconvenienced. An invitation to pop round has become the custom, but that is not how we grew up. Friends and family popped round without invitations, our hospitality was welcoming, and we shared our food and drink without hesitation. We all need our space. Our homes are our sanctuaries at times, so we can deal with the stresses and strains of modern-day life, but surely not to the point where our homes have become fortresses where only the invited are welcome. If you don't believe me about how our customs have changed, listen to these funny examples from fathers who admit to being a bit embarrassed:

- Friends not wanting to come to events because they had not received a personal invitation card although they were verbally invited.

- A father's sister deciding not to go to her family's Sunday dinner because her brother did not call to remind her. She admitted to remembering but was waiting for the verbal invitation.

- Looking through the curtains and not opening the door to one father's cousins because they had "just popped round" without informing him in advance.

- An uncle refusing to make a sandwich for his nephew who was hungry because he only had enough sandwich filling for his work sandwiches the next day.

- Not allowing friends round their houses until they were perfectly decorated and then treating their homes like master showpieces.

- Treating our homes with pride is good, but when family told three-year-old Daniel he should not come round because he may 'ruin the white carpets', it seems to be taking 'house-proud' a little too far.

These are some of the worst examples I was told, but I was also informed of some heartfelt stories. They illustrate a point about the thinking and attitude that can catch even the best of us off guard. Many fathers to whom I told these stories were initially shocked, but at the same time, they found them funny. This was replaced with thoughts of how life has really changed compared to when they were children. Some fathers could not believe family would treat each other in such a selfish way, whilst others said they knew of even worse examples than the ones mentioned.

Having traits from the major culture is not a crime; in fact, it can be positive in so many ways. Our everyday lives are consumed with customs, practices, and lifestyle decisions, such as visiting the DIY store, or they can be tribal, like an affinity for a football club, gardening, or the shopping mall experience. This includes other more specific activities such as practising your religion and political affiliation and our right to privacy.

There are also customs with which we struggle, such as allowing our pets to sleep in the bed as a part of the family and giving them a special diet. Treating a pet like a family member is unusual in African and Caribbean households where a dog is simply a dog, but such practise is what makes Britain the country it is. You may not agree with it but accept a person's right to choose to live within the laws of the land. Choice and a balance between our Caribbean and African cultures provide us with a rich cultural mix, and it can be so liberating to exist between the two as it includes choices such as what types of food to eat, where to go on holidays, what types of clothes to wear, and what language to speak at a given time. Adapting to different cultural customs is positively healthy as you get the best of both worlds, but it should not be at the expense of the extended family model.

A father spoke about his cultural experience at school. His friendship group was mixed, with Black, white and Indian friends. He had visited both his Asian and English homes and experienced different customs, as did they. He fondly remembered talking with them about their favourite foods.

His white friends spoke about chips, mashed potatoes, shepherd's pie, puddings, and stew. His Indian friends spoke about naan bread, tandoori chicken, and sweets. He spoke about rice 'n' peas, chicken, plantain, ackee, and saltfish. They were curious about each other's foods and were able to taste them by visiting each other's homes.

This father's experience is the perfect example of how you can enhance and enrich your family's ways of life with parts of other cultures. Many throughout the generations have done so, not just by combining food into their daily lives but also by practising other customs. For instance, fathers spoke about liking the basic values of the Asian – and parts of the African – continent's religious celebrations, like Diwali and Eid/Ramadan. Although they do not follow the fasting in the strictest sense, their families do spend periods fasting to appreciate what they have in life compared to others.

Does the extended family need saving?

The pitfalls experienced by fathers moving far or strategically to certain areas is that it makes it difficult for both the old and young to visit them. Yes, by all means, buy that dream house you've always dreamed of having, but try to make a strategic decision that will allow you to provide an open door to welcome your extended families, welcoming both old and young. That is, of course, unless you really need to get away from your family to preserve your sanity.

Once people are able to better themselves, invariably they look for better quality housing, environments, and schools for their children. The advantage can be that others will follow, and before you know it, you will have like-minded neighbours from different ethnic backgrounds who share similar educational and social aspirations to you. You may believe that, in some ways, it was the right decision, but it's not in other ways.

We are now a part of the older generation (grandparents, parents, aunts, and uncles), and we can recreate, to some extent, the extended families in which we had the privilege to play and live. Its function also includes absorbing all the punches modern life throws at us. Supporting each other in our daily lives, for things such as childcare, can be one of the areas in which we can try to improve. We can still win all round, even if your move was not strategic enough, if you are willing to put some effort into recreating the support system you once had. I hear people talk about community spirit and how they would like to see it return because they want a sense of belonging and shared investment in their family and local community. This cannot be a bad thing as human beings have a natural instinct for that sense of belonging. Some areas have an annual street party or event for neighbours to get to know each other and build community spirit and an environment in which families feel safe.

Most fathers I spoke to do not believe that the romantic notion of the extended family works for all British families. Even during our childhoods, there were family mavericks who only turned up on their terms or not at all. Some fathers spoke about trying to get their families to meet more often but realised that not all of their brothers and sisters had a similar mindset or needed to be closer as families, whilst others made it clear they had always been close and met their extended families on a regular basis.

Hopefully, any difficulties with adult family members do not prevent your children's cousins from meeting up and playing together. After all, it is not the children's fault if their parents can't see eye to eye!

> **Father:** 'I do not get on too tough (well) with my brother, but our children see each other quite often. We understand the value of them knowing and playing with their cousins as we used to as kids.'

This is a part of the battle if you decide to continue to be a part of your extended family. I see the importance of holding on and working to ensure the extended family continues to exist for all concerned. There is a lot of discussion in the community, in the media, and politically, as to the absence of father figures for some Black boys. Their safety, protection, and upbringing are the duty of their family but also the extended family and community. This network of safe havens is to guide them through teenage and early adult life. In the cultures where a generational hierarchy of advice and support exists, the young seem to be more settled and have a sense of belonging. Lessening the need for our sons to seek a substitute family for safety and protection, such as gang affiliation. Our extended families are a part of who we are, our past, present, and future. Our immediate families are shrinking due to our having fewer children, so we need to ensure that our children can identify and value their wider family networks. We can, however, start small to remember the habits of sharing, community, cooperation, and interdependency while there are still generations who remember what it was like to have a safe haven.

From Boyhood to Manhood: Helping Your Son to Grow Up the Right Way

'The apple never falls far from the tree.'
– Ralph Waldo Emerson

This chapter was supposed to be about parenting teenagers, the challenges we face as fathers, and self-help advice from our fellow fathers. However, as I spoke to fathers about their challenges when guiding their sons to make the right decisions in life against outside influences, I realised the importance of how a fathers' masculine identity can either support or impede their sons' development. In short, do you want your son to be the mirror image of you?

Fatherhood and masculinity: modern day challenges

Some fathers can sense something is seriously wrong. Research and the news focus on men of colour experiencing depression, poor mental health, homelessness, inequity in policing stops and searches, inequity in the judicial system and sentencing, disproportionate young men in prison, disproportionate cautions on our records that affect our sons' abilities to apply for certain jobs, the rise in fatal stabbings among gang and non-gang teenagers and suicide among men of colour, which continues to rise at an alarming rate.

> **Terrance:** 'Their experience with the establishment (nursery workers, teachers, the media, and the police in the first instance and in the wider public, shop keepers, employers, shop security guards, and bus drivers just some named by fathers) can either confirm, confuse, or in extreme cases, damage a young persons' inner confidence, because they are treated with suspicion.'

The issue of masculinity is complex and intertwined within history, culture, tradition, and gender pressures of what society expects of men and what we expect of ourselves. The impact of our masculine existence and the parenting of our sons are at a critical point in Britain. If we don't start to talk to each other about the destructive nature of our masculine existence and how it affects our parenting by sometimes blindly contributing to its continuation and look for solutions, it will lead to our sons' downfalls, and our sons are likely to become nothing but statistics.

It is likely that our attitudes towards gender roles and parenting will be passed – either consciously or unconsciously – to our children through our everyday behaviour. Our swagger showing our masculinity and that we can cope with any challenges life throws at us, to our friends, families, and the outside world negatively or positively having an impact on our relationships with our sons' and daughters' development. Would letting go of parts of our negative (I discuss these later in the chapter) masculine upbringing lead to us being better fathers? Does our masculine behaviour around suppressing our emotions hinder or assist communication with our sons who need us to manoeuvre through what are subtle – and at times, hostile – paths in life? If, as fathers, we cannot explain or guide our sons in what lies ahead, they are likely to fall into one of the traps that await them.

These are big questions that have taken up a lot of time in the groups and with the individual men to whom I have spoken. I think you will find the thoughts and feelings of fathers revealing. At times, their comments may sound controversial, but we are dealing with what I consider to be heightened emotional states of debate and topics that explore the very nature of man. Many have not had the opportunity to talk about such a sensitive topic – about the essence of who they are and how they came to be – before. You may or may not agree with some of the comments you are about to read, but they nevertheless make for fascinating reading.

Breaking down masculinity

What does it mean to be masculine? There are many layers to answering this question, but if we are to understand the danger we face as men and that our sons are likely to face, certain characteristics stand out when I think about the discussions with the fathers that explain why our very existence needs talking about. Below are some common characteristic that define masculinity you may have personally experienced or can relate to.

- **Men's physical strength and our egos.** How often do we exhibit strength in our homes, such as moving pieces of furniture, DIY projects, opening difficult jars, playing sports, or lifting weights at our local gym? As men, we seem to have no difficulty talking about or showing off our masculine physiques to each other or any women who are prepared to listen. Some men view having muscles – the modern-day six-pack stomach – as a validation of their maleness because it confirms their physical prowess over other men. You may have noticed that some smaller men tend to compensate for their lack of height by bodybuilding to increase body mass and feel stronger and less inadequate.

- Central to male masculinity is the **suppression of our vulnerable emotions, especially uncertainty.** The showing of emotions is seen by many men as being weak. I have witnessed male friends refusing to back down in heated topical disagreements even when it is obvious to everyone, they are wrong. How many times have you watched a film at home or in the cinema and felt water in your eyes due to a sad moment in the film that touches you? You may feel like crying, but you cannot allow yourself to cry – after all, what would people think of you? What would you think of yourself? How many of us openly admit to feeling fragile or vulnerable at a given time or uncertain about a decision we have made or an action we are about to take? A high majority of fathers thought that a public show of emotion or uncertainty in a situation might be viewed by others as being weak and having no place in the life of a strong, self-assured man of colour.

- **Economic independence** defines our masculinity in the workplace and is another important area that defines us as men. In particular, the 'breadwinner' family model can lead to men's abilities to financially control their households and make important financial decisions.

A lot of men have been programmed to be in control of their own destinies, both in the workplace and in the home. The workplace can provide an arena for exercising strong independent traits by performing in a competitive manner. In the right workplace, such traits can win acknowledgement for their hard work, receive pay raises, or the ultimate reward of promotions. A man's self-worth in the main still seems to be very much centred on his ability to work. Therefore, structural inequality can hinder progression and/ or promotion, and prolonged unemployment has been known to affect the confidence and self-esteem of men who believe their function is to provide for their families. I personally know of men who have taken their lives because they have felt a deep sense of inadequacy due to unemployment.

Ironically, there is a rise in British men becoming househusbands, but the majority of fathers I have met feel this trend goes against their masculine male identities, as there is the strong desire to work. However, as discussed in the chapter, **So Your Woman Earns More Than You!**, times are changing with the rise of highly qualified and confident women entering the workplace and taking more of a lead in financial decision-making at work and in the home.

- **Our intense interest in sexual conquest can define us in the social arena.** You only need to be in a pub or wine bar on a Friday night to witness this topic in its flow. The stereotype of men of colour as testosterone-driven predators are still viewed by some men as a part of their natural make-up. Our need for sex is wrapped up in our masculine identities and goes to, once again, confirm our manliness. You need look no further than the importance of developing our 'chat-up' lines to woo the opposite sex, but the destructive opposite is men who decide that sexual conquest as their main treatment of women is disrespectful and cold.

> **Cecil:** 'Whether you have had sex or not as a teenager, you are not allowed to say, "I'm a virgin," to your friends as you risk being seen as a wimp. So many teenage boys will brag about their sexual conquests and their staying power when, in fact, they have not managed to get past masturbation yet. The pressure to "score" is huge among teenage boys and young men, but how come? Where do they learn this from? Society, friends, uncles, and their dads.'

Some boys rush into having sex before they truly understand the responsibility and consequences. They can become fathers before they have even thought about wanting to be one, but the rush to get sex over with for the first time and be able to tell their friends is, at times, greater than the actual sexual act. Britain has the highest statistics for teenage pregnancy in Europe, and there are many reasons for this.

- **Society supports destructive masculine traits in popular culture:** music, films, magazines, and products for men. For men of colour, the stereotyping is quite stark and narrow, exploiting the image that we are all involved in crime, gangs, womanising, having a lot of children with different women, violent, remorseless, uneducated, lazy, and in low paid jobs. If we do succeed, it is only in creative fields, such as music and sports.

The uncomfortable truth

Phew. So, there you have it! Even before we start talking about how to parent our sons, it seems that we have all these challenges with which to contend. If we can be honest with ourselves, looking at the above list, we have all, at some time, played our part, either consciously or unconsciously, promoting these male traits.

> **Daniel:** 'All of the above at some time in my life. Well, not the crime side – that's a path that I never considered. It's scary to see it on paper because find me a positive in any of those definitions – what are we doing to ourselves?'

> **Shola:** 'Hold on... hold on – the strength and muscle definition. I spent a lot of time when I was young building my muscles. I don't think that was detrimental to me. It gave me a strong body and a strong mind. When I think about it, I did feel strong, like Superman, almost invincible. It was important, as a Black man, to be strong because if we are not, society will chew us up and spit us out. So, I don't agree with physique and strength being an issue. My son is lean because he is working towards his karate black belt. He doesn't have muscle bulk but is a physical specimen. That's not to show off, but to be able to protect himself and his family from the racists out there.'

> **Daniel:** 'I get your point: protecting our families is important, but there are men who use the strength against their partners,

like punching them, using their strength to control their women. That's so out of order. That's what I think the definition is getting at. My sister's ex punched her. We went round and beat him up and threw him out. It's my sister's house, and he is punching her in her own house?'

Samuel: 'You look at domestic violence, gangs, fighting, stabbings, genocide, wars around the world... it's all men spreading the violence, so there is a deeper part of masculinity that shapes us to be violent.'

Of the majority of men I met, this was the first time they discussed masculinity. Masculinity is like a tradition – no one can put a date on it, but it's important to follow because everyone else is, without question. The cultural celebration in public and private reinforces to men throughout their lives the importance of their gender's superiority. Some men have gone as far as saying that we have lost our way as men because we blindly follow a gender-specific role that is destructive towards us and our abilities to be role models to our sons. One thing about which the fathers were clear from the onset was that men do not sit around, talking about their masculinity and what it means to them in everyday life, and how the definition and expectations of being masculine have affected them and their families is not something men are accustomed to talking about openly.

Emmanuel: 'It's not like we get up one morning, look in the mirror, and think, I'm a man – how can I show my masculinity to the world today? It's just not something we do.'

Kwasi: 'After my friend told me about how he tackled a complicated plumbing job, he doesn't end the conversation by saying, "That was very masculine of me, wasn't it?" We talk a lot but not about whether being masculine is good or bad for us. It is something I have thought about in private, not with my friends. That would feel uncomfortable.'

These comments highlight certain common themes: the desire for some men to behave in such a prescribed masculine way throughout their lives without questioning the flipside to physical strength and the destructive power it can have over some women; suppressing our feelings; the destructive nature of closing down emotionally and not talking about our thoughts and feelings; the importance of sexual conquests that can lead to unwanted pregnancies and broken relationships; the eroding effects of structural inequality that grinds down our spirit and self-worth to progress in the workplace and realise our talents.

Some argue that society has rapidly changed over the last 30 years whilst men have struggled to adapt to new demands placed on them within the home and the rise in educated and professional women entering the workplace. These women want a more fluid gender role approach in their relationships and parenting. Some men have adapted. A partnership between the sexes that compliments the shared work and home life responsibilities is now seen as the preferred gender balance, rather than the old, traditional, breadwinning male of work, coming home to a cooked meal on the table. It's a bit crude, but you get the picture.

However, the majority of men I met seem to be hesitant or refuse to change, wanting things to remain the same. Although not explicitly said, I sense these men are fearful that even small changes might render their masculine identities learned from their fathers less significant today.

Creatures throughout history have adapted to survive their changing environments, and although some men have, a lot of us struggle to share the responsibilities of work, home, and childcare. There are a lot of wives and partners who literally give a superhuman effort at work, home, and during childcare to ensure the home ticks over and functions rather than leave things to their husbands. I hear these women talking; some talk to me through frustration as they yearn for some assistance from their husbands.

Don't get me wrong. These women love their men dearly, and they acknowledge they may have 'spoilt' their men along the way before the children were born, but they recognise that the modern-day pressures of life are fast-paced, and the need to share gender roles has become urgent; otherwise, we run the risk of been seen as burdens within our families rather than assets.

The need for men to adapt is not lost on some fathers I have met, but so many fathers are hard-wired from an early age to be traditional men. Thankfully, we have a beginning, a chink in armour of the unbending attitude around gender roles – and in particular, masculine roles – taught to us from a very young age.

The uncomfortable truth about which Kwasi speaks is that the majority of the fathers took a while to switch-off from our male-masking behaviours. Our masking is part of our learnt behaviour about showing that everything is okay even if it is not and that we are in control of our lives and the situations around us as men do not want to be viewed as weak or unmanly. It took some established groups in which trust had been developed to get past the masking, the delays, and awkward moments to talk subjectively and openly about their experiences without feeling they would be judged in a negative light.

In order to understand how our masculine upbringings have moulded us into the men and fathers we are today, we need to embrace and understand the past to address the present and adapt to the modern-day parenting of our sons.

'Big boys don't cry': early recollections of masculine programming

Without exception, all the fathers recalled the moment they were either told or discouraged from crying. The message was that 'big boys don't cry'. This was the beginning – or you could say the rite of passage – into manhood. Being brave when grazing your knee, not crying, and holding your emotions in – being masculine – was just the tip of the iceberg. Within our cultures, the control of our emotions is buried deep within our male DNA, to be strong and fearless even if we may not feel that way inside.

Our need and will to survive hostile environments have been well-documented throughout history, and it can make us paranoid about being seen as masculine and in control of our environments. After all, the strongest survive, so we can overcompensate for being masculine and teach these lessons to the younger males in our family because our instincts tell us this is the way to be, the way to survive. This is one aspect, among others, that have protected us from danger and totally distinguish our ability to look pain and fear in the eyes, brush them off, and move on. I cannot even describe to you the realisation this prompted within the groups and individuals to which I spoke.

The surge in energy level as the fathers swivelled in their seats to share common experiences from their largely untold boyhood stories of growing up in Britain and how their boyhood experiences have caused internal tensions with the move towards the so-called modern man. This starts with the consistency of the message to stop crying, which became more regular from the age of five. As one father explained,

> **Yemi:** 'One minute it was okay to cry, and the next it wasn't. I remember grazing my elbow. It hurt, but I was clearly told by my dad in a stern voice to stop crying. This happened several times, so I started to learn to control my feelings inside of me and take the pain. I didn't bother my dad again.'

The discouragement of the use of tears to express our feelings was identified by some fathers as the first step towards being programmed into their masculine roles as being tough and unemotional. Another father talked about falling over during a football match and hurting his knee:

> **Jeff:** 'I was clearly in pain, but I did not want anyone to notice my pain. I was about nine years old, and I wanted to scream out with pain, but I was fearful of being called names like sissy. I learned at an early age to keep my pain and my hurt to myself, just like the older males in my family do.'

At one stage or another, we have all received either direct or indirect messages from our friends, family, and the wider community that crying is a sign of emotional weakness in boys, so we obliged and stopped exhibiting this emotion. Interestingly, Jeff recollected being hit by a football in the testicles as a teenager and rolling around in agony, so it seems to be deemed okay to wallow in pain because we can all sympathise and know how painful such an impact can be.

Whilst girls are allowed to show their emotions, boys' emotional development still continues to be under surveillance by family members and the wider community. One father stated that it was a lonely place having to internalise his emotion when it had previously been okay to show his emotions. He seemed to speak with hurt whilst recalling the occasion when he went to hug his father:

> **Mohamed:** 'My father was sitting on a chair, and I went to hug him, and he moved away and said to me that I was a bit old for a hug now. That was it. I wasn't allowed to hug my dad anymore. It felt like a rejection of my love, and from that moment, we never hugged

again. At the time, I was confused, but I now know what he was trying to do: teach me to not need hugs as a boy to make me strong.'

I could see the hurt on Mohamed's face as he recalled the moment and acknowledged that the incident was a defining moment for him as a boy. He learned to control his emotions towards other boys and men, but interestingly, was able to continue hugging his mother and female family members.

My recollection

My scenario was slightly different as my dad just did not do hugs... ever. I remember him allowing me to sit on his lap when I had tonsillitis and fever, and I remember feeling safe and secure, but due to my build, my dad and uncles had nicknamed me 'heavyweight champion'. At the time, heavyweight boxing was popular, and Cassius Clay (later to be renamed Mohamed Ali) was the new kid on the block. As I watched Mohammed Ali on TV, I felt like Superman, like I could beat up anyone. My family told me I was strong and possessed a hard punch, so I believed them, and my boyhood masculinity was set.

My masculinity within my family was confirmed at an early age, about seven or eight years old. That meant I stopped receiving the usual hugs from my uncles. Instead, they greeted me with playful, sparring jabs that reinforced my toughness. I was not aware of the change, nor did I understand its significance at the time.

On reflection, I preferred the hugs, piggybacks, and being swung around rather than sparring punches. However, my world was about to come to a turning point. Whilst mimicking the heavyweight champion of the world at school, I accidentally punched one of my friends in the face, and his mouth started to bleed. I was shocked to see the blood and hear him crying out loud.

At that instant, I realised that boxing was no longer fun for me if it included hurting a friend. I told one of my uncles what had happened at school and announced my retirement from boxing. He was not amused and advised me to carry on as no one would pick on me at school, and he was not at all concerned for my friend. Needless to say, I soldiered on as a champion-in-waiting to please the male side of my family, but deep down, I knew it was not for me. Not having emotions was not for me.

> **Phillip:** 'My father regularly told me as a boy to "man up", be a man, and go and fight the boy at school who was picking on me. My father was not happy with me being seen as weak and ordered me to stick up for myself. That phrase, "man up", has never left me. To this day, I use it to tell myself when things are going against me and I need to stick out my chest and be a man. Or, if I feel my sons are being too soft, I tell them to "man up" – see? There I go again! I use it when I feel they need to be tough. You can't let people walk all over you.'

I could recite so many other stories I have been told, but the stories have a similar message for us, piercing through our hearts as boys when it was time to grow up, put our feelings aside, and start living up to the expectations of being men of colour. The need for affection from other male family members was no longer available to us, and the message was that it was time to suppress our emotions and become stronger for it.

By all means, we could still receive affection and hugs from our mothers and other females. That was acceptable due to their perceived nurturing roles. It was not that we did not want to seek out our male family members, but it was the unspoken word that you no longer sought out their emotional or physical comfort. Dads and other males had become no-go areas in relation to emotional contact.

Is masculinity killing us?

As fathers, we shared stories of our earliest recollections of being encouraged or programmed to be masculine. Some of the fathers are still hurt, and they can link it to learning to control their emotions. Many admitted to feeling emotionally 'boxed in' by what was expected of them and the confusion of what they expected of themselves as boys and as men today. The times in which we grew up, in the '60s, '70s, '80s, and '90s, the male culture surrounding men of colour was and still is very masculine in nature. There was a very clear division of gender roles between the sexes. The exhibiting of one's maleness as a teenager and/or adult was based on the clothes one wore, the way one walked, talked, and behaved, one's ability to attract women, being able to 'hold' one's drink, and being the breadwinner within one's family.

Your ego or self-assured presence was always on the surface, played out in public whether you felt that way or not. As a boy, you initially learned, through your teenage years and into adulthood, to mask the true feelings you did not want others to see. You could have had a very emotional day filled with hurt, but no one would know. Here lie some of the difficulties with men. Our ways of life from boyhood to adulthood have – and continue at times to be – emotionally destructive ways of living. Although, at times, we feel emotionally 'boxed in' by the way we perceive we are expected to behave, we continue to live life in ways that may be dangerous for our long-term health and our families' happiness.

Father: 'Guys, we need to be close to our sons. Hug them, tell them we love them, and talk about racism, the streets, and the injustices we face so they it can be guided. Let's not be like many fathers, closed to talking about these things. We know it's tough out there for our sons, so firmness and showing we care should be in equal measures because that's how we get them through the prejudices and hate they are facing out there so that they can achieve whatever their dreams are in life.'

The evidence of our masculine behaviours being destructive for our wellbeing has built up over a number of decades, and if left unchecked, can eventually literally kill us! Here are a few chosen areas to make my point:

Teaching your teenager not to hate

My son supports Arsenal Football Club, and he has a club shirt. He idolises certain players that play for Arsenal and England. The mystique of the royal family used to enchant my daughter when she was younger and going through that princess stage. In other words, they are patriotic. It is fair to say that when England is playing sports, they shout the house down and always want them to win, no matter what. I watch them and feel good they have a connection with the country in which they were born. Their connections transcend colour or class because these issues are not yet at the forefront of their minds or experiences. Their connections are not rational decisions but emotional attachments to familiarity and their British identity. They identify with certain sports, the men and women who represent Britain and want them to do well. I asked my kids why they support England, and the reply was "Because we just do," but I also look at my children and know someone will test their patriotism, just like mine was tested by my first counter with the police, and the countless National Front gangs who tried to catch and beat me up. They never did – I wasn't the fastest kid on the block, but those heavy Doc Marten boots they wore weren't made for running.

Our children will reach a defining moment in their lives when someone in the so-called establishment will – either directly or indirectly – make them feel like they do not belong, make them feel like outsiders due to the colour of their skin. Our children will start to ask questions such as, why do people hate us, or why do people say horrible things to me, like why don't you go back to Africa or where you come from? They may also wonder at the way shopkeepers treat them and their friends as if they are going to steal something from their shops. Our children's natural reactions to such negative, and at times, hostile, comments will be the desire to argue or fight back because they feel vexed and personally insulted. I cannot tell you exactly what advice you should give your son as it will depend on the situation in which he finds himself and the danger he faces.

What we can say with certainty is that all fathers have been there at some time in their lives, and I'd bet you can remember how you've dealt with these situations. A lot of fathers said they learned to deal with discrimination as a teenager through trial and error but mainly by exhibiting a lot of anger, and at times, violence, towards the perpetrator, or emotionally withdraw, becoming hardened towards the country we thought loved us. Our children have to be careful as the rate of criminal records being given by the courts to Black teenagers means their future career choices can be seriously affected. Draw on your experiences so you can pass on to your children what worked for you.

My experience with racism was not just the subtle build-up of an incident here and an incident there that trickled down and eventually led to my eruption of anger. My teenage experience was a period of great race relations' upheaval within establishments that had negative attitudes towards ethnic minority groups. This was the time of the 'Sus' law, whereby police could stop and search you anywhere and at any time, and that meant that if you were Black, chances were you would be regularly stopped and searched. In a one-month period, I had been stopped 9 times, searched, arrested (twice for objecting to being searched), and punched a few times in my head in the back of the police SPG van for being 'arrogant for thinking I knew my rights.' We had to listen to degrading and racist comments from some policemen wanting a response to give them a reason to arrest us. At the time, the streets were a scary place to be, but ironically, the streets were also playgrounds where we met, debated, and had fun together.

We knew our enemy then by the uniforms they wore and the fact that we did not share the same skin colour. You could see your enemy coming, giving you time to act and defend yourself physically or verbally before you were seized upon and caged in a police cell like an animal.

I was in the thick of things, attending many marches and demanding equality for all ethnic groups from all quarters of society. I, along with others my age, considered ourselves intellectual warriors who could communicate the feelings of the Black community to others. We left the fighting to others, and the Brixton Riots and other uprisings around the country typified the feelings of our generation towards the establishment. Many felt that deprivation, high rates of youth unemployment, discrimination in the workplace and society, and police youth harassment were causes worth fighting for. To do nothing was to gain nothing. Our intellectual fight strategies were to win the hearts and minds of the public to our plight and our heroes who guided us, like Martin Luther King, Gandhi, and Mandela, all revered men who showed us that victory did not come by using the sword but by using words. We felt like international freedom fighters. The fight for justice was not just about me but all of my South African brothers who fought against Apartheid, and like Nelson Mandela, many of us were willing to go to jail for what we believed in.

But I did not hate the police. Why? Because my parents did not have hate in their souls; therefore, I did not witness the cancer of hate and desperation that other families had in their homes. What I did learn within my family was religious-based, to turn the other cheek and try to forgive wrongdoings. At times, when confronted by the police on another dark street filled with a sea of blue uniforms rippling through the midnight air, ready to sweep us away in a violent wave of force, I felt both fear and pity for the officers. I could see that they hated me. I could see the hate in their eyes towards a person whose name they did not know. I could see they hated my colour, my hair, my clothes, and my accent. I could feel they hated my being in the country they considered theirs by the name-calling I experienced like a cold dagger in my chest. The words hurt, but I could not hate them because my family had taught me not to hate another human being, irrespective of our differences. I understood that hate is a negative state of mind, devoid of goodness and growth. Hate is a powerful emotion that can consume a person and cloud their judgement, moving them further away from humanity. I understood and knew people who had lost generations of their families in terrible wars. I understood why they would have cause to hate their enemies, but when you ask racists why they hate you, they struggle to answer because their feelings of hate have dominated their reasoning for so long; they forget why and how their hate started. Invariably, their answers are along the lines of, 'You've taken our house,' or 'You've taken our jobs,' or 'You've taken our women.' There is no mention of murdering or hurting any of their family or friends. To hate us if we have committed atrocities against your families, I would, shamefully, understand and beg for your forgiveness but not over bricks and mortar, employment opportunities, relationships, or just because you want to. I realised that I had to hang on for dear life to a system that wanted to rid itself of so many of us.

I had to contend with two racist policemen every morning on my way to school. They would sit there, parked in their police car every morning. They would call me over by using derogatory words, questioning whether I was really on my way to school or up to no good. Their every word stripped off another layer of my skin until I became transparent and felt naked for all to see. My boyhood innocence where race and colour were concerned had gone, and I'd had enough. I sought refuge and advice from my father, and to my amazement, he told me to always remain calm, polite, and courteous by saying, 'Good morning, officers.' I was gobsmacked as I'd expected a different response from my dad, something like, 'Let's man up and go and sort this mess out.' My dad taught me some valuable lessons that day: to choose my fights carefully, how to deal with discrimination, and how not to react when being pushed as retaliation often lands the victim in trouble, and the perpetrator walks free.

As a teenager, I was at a crossroads at which so many my age had found themselves. Some decided to say goodbye to the state and goodbye to the establishment, goodbye to the love affair that had started as innocent boys, wearing England's football shirt and screaming for their heroes to succeed so they would all succeed and feel the pride we willed them as one united country full of patriotism. The reason behind this is that the love affair that had taken us to such emotional heights was not reciprocated, and although I was in denial for so long, believing that everything would be okay if I just wished it to be, it was undeniable that things would never be the same.

> **Jeff:** 'The constant stop and search to me and my spars friends compared to my white friends was so obvious. I know the police did not like me. Hell, I didn't like them either.'

The advice my dad gave me only works for given situations, and it will not work for everyone as we have different personalities and attitudes, but what the fathers felt was important to any situation, irrespective of who they were. If you allow the person to know how to press your inner destruct button whereby you would be in such a rage that your actions could end up getting you into trouble with the law or any other establishment at which you work or study, then it was unlikely to be the right response, as you would no longer be in control of your actions, and the person would know this and press your button at will.

Like my dad did for me all those years ago guided me to not lose my cool, you will find yourself having to guide your son through these difficult times, in which their patriotism and their sense of belonging will be tested. Most importantly, we must teach our sons how not to allow others to influence how we feel about ourselves and not to doubt our abilities and talents.

Your guidance will set the scene for how they deal with future confrontations and whether they turn their backs on or continue to embrace the country in which they were born. The fact is that, when I think about it, my dad was teaching me to 'man up' by sending me to face the two policemen. I can tell you that it was scary, but it was my initiation into a world in which some people just do not like us. He must have had the faith in me that I was strong enough to handle the situation by myself. There will come a time when we will all have to let our sons fend for themselves, not because we do not care but because they will need to learn to stand on their own two feet.

> **Ali:** 'You can end up hating the very country you were born in because of the way we were treated, but my family endured a lot, and my parents never allowed me to hate. They always told me that we tend to remember the bad situations rather than the many, many good situations with the people we meet. So, thankfully, this is what I pass on to my children. I just view some police and shopkeepers that watch my sons as if they are going to steal something as ignorant as my children know not to take things that do not belong to them.'

The anger, which usually starts as a justified feeling due to injustice, can be used positively when channelled to show others what you can achieve despite all the systemic inequality. However, it can also change to hate and consume, paralyse, and become lost in time as the years pass and the hate simmers, waiting for the moment to explode. In addition, these angry sons could get into a lot of trouble, making them victims of the time, unable to forgive or move on with their lives.

We need to teach our teenagers to balance their good experiences with the bad rather than let the bad experiences dominate their daily thoughts and actions. The consequences of not doing so are readily seen in our young being over-represented in the judicial system and gang membership and disproportionately stopped and searched.

I acknowledge this is a simplistic explanation for a complicated issue that also includes the absent fathers' roles. Absent fathers need to be involved so that they can share their experiences.

Furthermore, re-establishing contact with their sons is essential as some of the anger directed at them for not being around to support and guide them through feelings of not belonging need to be resolved.

We must teach our sons not to hate and encourage them to have healthy and balanced outlooks in life, even when they are being tested, because the majority of people with whom they will come into contact are likely to be kind. To hate is a losing approach in any situation in life. I have yet to meet a person who hates someone or the world who is content and happy from within.

We cannot address our sons' issues if we do not become aware of how our own masculine existences can hinder our parenting of them and our own feelings of being unwelcome as teenagers, so some fathers I met have built their armour around suppressing their feelings and not being open with our sons about how scary it is out there to be a person of colour. Some fathers use their swagger as if nothing bothers us, and we can solve everything by ourselves because we are all-conquering males. We give the impression that's it's okay to be womanisers, father multiple children from different partners, and be strangers to our children. We are cool when we promote the media's expectation and money-making Black culture of excessive spending on clothes, cars, raves, and drink, all to look good to others rather than have long term financial portfolios for our children to prosper in the future.

I wish my parents had shared with me their experiences of racism whilst I was growing up, but I know my mum didn't because she did not want us to hate as hate is un-Christian. They wanted us to be educated, to integrate and fight structural inequalities from within that ensure people of colour do not remain in dead-end employment, allowing privileged board members and their families to maintain their destinies and wealth. At the time, I was just an angry teenager without a plan, but I get it now. What I have learned and passed onto my children is the importance of staying calm under pressure and not allowing people to get under your skin and doubt their untapped talent that every child is born with, but just need the positive encouragement and unwavering guidance to untapped I remember a youth worker advising me that being stopped by the police is like a chess game. If you are arrested, you are in a position of checkmate, and the game is over, you have lost, but if you walk away, you have won the chess game and live to fight another day. My message to my son is not to allow himself to be checkmated in conflict situations through his anger. So, maybe my parents in their own way did not see the benefit in sharing their experiences if they felt they did not have the tools to show us how to deal with the hostility they encountered in the UK.

However, we have the advantage our parents did not have. We are born into and continue to experience and understand subtle systems that squeezes us gently like a phantom snake in all walks of life, sucking the life out of our body and mind. The more you struggle, the less air you are able to breath; the more you wriggle, the less space you have to escape. Until you are so tired you stop fighting, accepting that your talents are unlikely to be realised or supported, so you settle for less, just to survive.

I cannot help thinking that saying forewarned is forearmed, and it may have saved us fathers a lot of painful experiences and feelings of being unwanted by the country into which we were born. Unfortunately, our parents may not have had the time or energy to decipher their own experiences to prepare us better to avoid emotional and physiological traumas through which many have gone through and continue do so. We all have stories These experiences all reconfirm how we are treated differently and how we can be treated in a discriminatory manner due to our skin colour. It is during the teenage years that we develop a sixth sense for identifying people who do not like us, not because of our character or personality, but because of the colour of our skin. This vital stage is where, as a teenager, I witnessed school friends' inner-confidence evaporate, so much that they became paranoid and developed conspiracy theories around race for every interaction they experienced. This can be debilitating for some, and they carry it into adulthood, whereby they continue to blame others for their plights in life, living on benefits from the state and without dreams for which to aim.

> **Desmond:** 'I use to wear my England shirt when I was a youngster, and like most boys, I dreamt of playing for England, but that goes when all you hear on the news is negative things about your community and about your colour. At school, you know certain teachers didn't like or believe in you you and shop security always treated you like a criminal. Don't even get me started on the police and football hooliganism that had racism flowing through their veins! It's like a drip-drip effect on your self-esteem and ability to thrive. Everything that goes wrong in Britain is blamed on us, and eventually, you just stop your dream of playing for England, and reality hits you that you are not wanted here no matter how hard you work or try to fit in. You stop being patriotic because deep down, you know you are not wanted and not liked. It's not always what people say, it's their actions of being overlooked for promotion or additional training to better yourself and the looks you get that you

know what they are thinking. You know that they don't really want you here, and you know that I don't want to be here either.'

These are strong feelings from one father that I believe illustrates the point of having to almost grow a thick skin and not let the minority of hate mongers dictate your life. Later in this chapter, we talk about how to boost your sons' and daughters' inner confidence, no matter your ethnicity, and the importance of culture in laying a solid foundation that will allow your children to feel proud of who they are, cementing their inner confidence and assisting them to deal not only with discrimination but also whatever challenges life throws at them. People in the public eye talk about having to grow thick skins especially in the social media world we live in, because of the unkind comments they have to endure. As many famous people have said, if you listen to all the negativity, written or spoken about you, you will never leave your house again.

Image and Black boys

We need to return to the importance of image and peer group pressure on our teenagers to look and act a certain way. As an ex-youth counsellor, this is one of the biggest issues that seem to affect teenagers. Teenagers like to belong, and they will spend a lot of time doing just that. How things have changed over the last 30 years, as everyone seems to want to impress others with either what they possess or the way they look. It's not that past generations did not participate in these teenage rituals; it's just that it seems much more pronounced and with greater pressure with social media dominating our very existence. Privacy seems no longer an option if you want to be relevant socially and in your career.

We are living in an era that has become absorbed with self- and body-image, showing your wealth and what a good time you are having rather than intellectual abilities. It would seem the more accepted our teenage children's image is to their peers, the more they seem to accept who they are.

As some fathers explained, it's a tough lesson for teenagers to learn that the impact of getting the latest pair of trainers or mobile phone will only last for a while, but their personality, character and untappd talents will last for a lifetime. As parents, you manage the stereotyping and pressure on boys to have 'cool' images and how this can have a detrimental effect on their achievement at school or college if this narrow narrative is allowed to continue. We already know that Black teenage boys, in particular, struggle with educational achievement when compared to some other cultural groups.

> **Adrian:** 'We know that we cannot make our teenagers change their attitudes overnight because what their peers and the outside world think about them is all-important to them. My biggest fear is what they are willing to do to fit in even if they know it is wrong. Will they be strong and say no or go along with the crowd? Depending on what it is, such actions can ruin your life and your life's opportunities, that's what concerns me, but I trust them to make the right decisions. I suppose we can plant the seeds every now and then by reminding our kids that not all their friends will still be their friends in three to five years' time when school finishes. At their age, friends come and go.'

Crying over you – our emotional selves

Most of the fathers to which I spoke explained that if they need a shoulder to cry on, they would seek out their partners and/or wives or female family members as safe people with whom to share their feelings.

The fathers did not discount talking to their male friends about problems they were having, but they would draw the line at being tearful or crying. In fact, some fathers acknowledged that they have different levels of friendships. They would make judgements to decide to which male friend they would talk. A common way to make a decision seemed to be the length of time they had known the friend, which made it easier to discuss personal issues, but crying on another male friend's shoulder was out of the question for all the men I met, irrelevant of whether they had known the person for a long time or not.

There did not seem to be difficulty with men showing their emotions (see section: **Big boys don't cry: early recollections of masculinity**) to females compared to other men. This seemed to be based on their perceptions of women having nurturing roles within their family whilst growing up. There is still a definite suppression of emotions when confronting male friends, as the fathers were concerned about what their reactions would be and how it might affect their long-term friendships. As one father sadly summed up at the ending of a session:

> **Karl:** 'There is no way my male friends are coming crying to me about their problems. I would feel odd. They just wouldn't put me in that situation. If they did, I would have to tell him he needs to move away from me with that crying.'

Sexual conquest and its effects

The definition of masculinity being an intense interest in sexual conquest caused the most controversy and frustration, whether I spoke to groups or individual men. The messages they wanted to convey to everyone reading this book is they are sick and tired of the historical stereotyping that all Black men have large penises and uncontrollable appetites for sex, that they spend all their time 'hunting' for sex, and this is their main preoccupation in life. The sex industry blatantly plays to this sexual stereotyping and many other Black fantasies around penis size. The person does not matter, just the size of his penis and what he can do with it. The fathers I met felt such stereotyping insulting to their intelligence. A father in one of the groups I met who is known to be mild-mannered really got heated up over this topic.

The fathers did concede that some of our brothers are happy to play to this stereotype and not commit to any one woman as they enjoy their 'player' status. However, in doing so, this minority of men damage the image and reputation of all men. This naturally leads to suspicion from women towards men who approach them, believing all men to be 'players' when, in fact, most men's intentions are honourable, but because some women have experienced so many time wasters or uncommitted men in their travels, it is, at times, difficult know who is genuine.

> **Father:** 'Some guys really need to grow up and stop playing up to this penis stereotype as it affects us descent men who do not wish to be seen in such a selfish manner and have their existence determined by what is between their legs. I'm a thinking man, a caring man, but women can be wary and believe the hype rather than seeing the man they are talking to. I don't blame the women because they have probably come across such men and experienced their shallowness all the time, but it just makes it harder for genuine men to get by.'

If you're wondering what this has to do with our sons, it has everything to do with them, as society and their fathers may have helped perpetuate this image of Black men, and in doing so, pass the message on to their sons that it's okay to leave a trail of women angry at their lack of commitment, to walk around and boast about their conquests, showing no respect for their victims. This is why it's good to hear fathers talk about the negative effects of sexual conquests on themselves and women.

Pressure on Black boys

Having spoken to so many fathers, what I have learned is how the media, the areas in which we live, and our families' upbringing affects us. This is particularly true of Black men who have a huge pressure placed on them by popular culture to be a certain type of male. The pressure from parts of society – and at times, internally – is for us and our sons to be cool and self-assured and not just sexually active but be really good at it. There is also pressure to be good at sports or in entertainment, spend our money on raves, have chauvinistic attitudes, and have relationships with women, purchase expensive clothes and fast cars, be fearless because we are so tough, we don't need to be loved, and to be individualistic, selfish, and anti-establishment. In fact, we should live in the fast lane by making money quickly (via illegal methods if all else fails) rather than through hard work, sacrificing to obtain good qualifications so we can eventually get good jobs. All of the above traits are the exact destructive behaviours we internalise as being acceptable within our male world that, in the end, leads to nowhere.

Black males have become the equivalent of what Hollywood would call being typecast. We play the same roles over and over again because we receive a strange type of positive acknowledgement from our audiences (peers, girlfriends, and the media) and start to believe that if we do not play these roles, we may fall into obscurity. The gender stress on us is overwhelming and wrong, and we need to understand that we are not here to please and entertain everyone. We can, at times, be too concerned about what other people think about us rather than what we think about ourselves in a form of colour-gender stress.

If we are to stop our boys from being typecast as the cool guys who are always ahead of the game in fashion, sports, cars, and music, we need to understand how gender pressure affects us. Allowing our boys to spend all of their money and time on the latest gear or mobile phones to look good rather than teaching them the art of opening a savings account and learning their roles within the family as young men only confirms this typecasting.

The roots of this can be found in some families where double standards in which their sons are allowed to 'play' for a large part of their boyhood and teenage years while not taking responsibility for chores within the home. Although girls in the family are expected to do chores at an early age, boys are not expected to take responsibility, so the message to young boys is to focus on things outside their home, expending their energy elsewhere rather than helping to build their usefulness within the home. This can later lead to grown men who have never learned how to take responsibility and understand that their roles within the family are not just about them and their needs but the importance of putting others' needs first. Here is an excerpt from a father who recounts how his dad's gambling directly affected his family whilst growing up:

> **Father:** 'I remember me and my sister being hungry as a child. At times, our mum went without so that we would not go to bed hungry. We didn't have a TV, so when our school friends talked about children's programmes, we couldn't join in. My dad was a gambler, and he used most of the money on that. My relationship with him is strained because he was and still is a selfish man. He was totally spoilt as a child. Being the only boy, he learned that his needs came first above everyone else, but he shouldn't use that as an excuse because we all make our choices in life. As an adult, I understand that when you have children, you must have the capacity to put your children before your own needs. So, I find it hard to respect him because he couldn't put us first before himself, so why bother to have kids if that's the way you are going to be?'

As fathers, we need to break this mould and guide our sons to have fun but balance this by focusing on their education and family lives before their peers; otherwise, they will start to believe a narrowly defined existence, not being open to finding other roles apart from what society or their peers expect of them. Our fears of being ordinary, of being just another guy and falling into obscurity is unlikely, as our talents are wide and varied, and at times, untapped. We can play other roles in society, like doctors, lawyers, editors, dentists, surveyors, MPs, managers, own our businesses, and even be professional ballet dancers if that is where our talents lie.

The ballet dancer

Ballet dancer? You have got to be kidding me, I hear you say. Well, I am totally serious. I want to tell you a quick story, although I appreciate that I am skimming over some important aspects of the story. It is about a man by the name of Carlos Acosta and how his dad's unconventional intervention saved him from a life of crime. Carlos's family lived in Cuba and was very poor. His father was a truck driver with 11 children and several mothers to support.

At the age of nine, Carlos was running wild on the streets of Havana. Carlos joined a breakdancing gang and dreamed of being a professional footballer. His dad was determined for Carlos to end his association with the gang, so he took drastic action by sending his son to a ballet school to learn discipline and keep him off the streets.

At first, Carlos hated the school, the type of traditional dancing, and the discipline, often getting into fights because his friends outside the ballet school called him a 'sissy'. Although Carlos had raw talent, his dance colleagues warned him that the establishment would never allow him to make it as a professional Black ballet dancer. Due to his perseverance, talent, and refusing to be typecast as just another Black street dancer, guess what? Carlos was one of the most renowned professional ballet dancers in the world. Having danced with companies like the National Ballet of Cuba, the English National Ballet and the American Ballet theatre. He is now the Director of Birmingham Royal ballet.

Why was this transformation possible for Carlos? Because his dad refused to allow his son to be typecast by following a narrow definition of what Carlos thought he would become in the future. His dad guided him from danger, out of the gang's activities, and showed him an alternative. At times, Carlos left the ballet school, only for his dad to send him back again. Once this hurdle was overcome, Carlos seemed to settle down, and the rest was down to Carlos.

Having to deal with leaving a very masculine, dangerous, and limiting life as a street gang member /breakdancer to a high cultural profession that has an under-representation of Black males and 'street cred' was difficult, but Carlos was able to rise above the negativity he faced both outside and internally. He realised he had a talent for ballet dancing, so he focused and put his energy into his eventual dream of becoming a professional ballet dancer. What people thought of him mattered – after all, he is human – but he realised that his dream was stronger than trying to please and be what others wanted him to be.

What intrigued some fathers (and buys into the myth of ballet dancers not being masculine) was whether Carlos had to develop his feminine side to become a professional ballet dancer, having come from a tough and very masculine street life. Let me answer the question like this: Carlos is probably, pound for pound, one of the fittest, athletic men in the world due to the rigorous training regime to which he commits. The body suppleness needed to perform his art form requires lifelong dedication. If you are still in doubt, why not challenge him to a 100-metre race, an endurance test, or a basic arm wrestle. It is unlikely you would beat him, and it is probable that he would not entertain your challenge, knowing that one's masculinity is not just about strength.

Carlos's story is a great example of thinking outside the box and not being typecast by your masculinity or allowing your son to be, either. So, the point is that our sons do not have to fit into the traditional box of just being cool, as this road leads to a dead end. Our contributions as fathers and teachers can guide our sons through difficult adolescent periods when expectations of them are low.

Fortunately, some fathers understand the importance of their sons finding their talents because they have gone through the blind alleys in life to ensure they spend their time and energy on perfecting their talents. Admittedly, my son Terrel is forging a career in the masculine sport of professional Rubgy. However, he has had to overcome his own challenges of being one of a few players who attended secondary school in an industry that is predominantly public school at the elite level. For those fathers who are new to fatherhood, this topic may be overwhelming, but it is invaluable learning and will put you in an even better position to understand gender pressure and guide your sons to realise their dreams and potentials, no matter how feminine or otherwise people might perceive their chosen professions to be.

Redefining masculine fatherhood

You may be reading this chapter and thinking that this sounds like a bit of doom and gloom; if we do not change as men, we risk extinction. What has happened to the positive messages about fathers sharing their thoughts with each other, growing, and improving our skills and knowledge as fathers? Well, that message is strong throughout the book, but there are times we must stop to reflect and question what is going on with us men around our masculine existences.

You may have felt this feeling deep down in your souls, that you feel boxed in by the way you are expected to act as males and know how to connect with your sons on a spiritual level. You initially felt this as a boy when you were encouraged not to show your emotions or cry when you were hurt. As an adult, you may have had feelings of uneasiness, that you were restricted to certain ways of behaving like a man, to compete with other men in the workplace, and to show you are in charge at home and anywhere else you end up at, not wanting to admit you are lost and feeling awkward, seeking directions when you are lost, seeking financial advisers for money-related matters, not confiding your fears to your partner in case she thinks less of you, not going to see your GP because you are meant to be like a Duracell battery with the capacity to go on and on without the need for medical intervention, not crying when you feel like it because you are concerned about what people would say and what you would think about yourself, after all, you are the man, right? In short, you feel like you are expected to have all the answers.

I could go on, but I think you get the idea about how we have learned how to be masculine and forgo our feminine sides because we were told at an early age that these are weaknesses to de discarded at the soonest opportunity. The fact of the matter is that it is far from being a weakness. It is a strength that we need to rediscover.

Don't get me wrong. This does not mean that the concept of masculinity is dead or useless. Believe me; it has its place because of its significance for the capitalist country in which we live, whereby competition and achievement are the cornerstones of the country and our need to survive.

What we need is to give ourselves a masculine choice. You see, the beautiful thing about Britain is that we have the ability to talk about these issues, choose the types of masculine behaviour we want to follow, and inform our sons, so they have the information to make informed masculine choices, just like Carlos was able to. As someone once said, you can make children but not their minds. So, let's try to help them to make wise choices.

Father: 'This has been a lot to take in. I don't agree with all the areas about masculinity, but I can see areas I can make changes in. Without going into detail, the emotional thing and opening up to my son, I will look at.'

Anthony: 'Wow, the bits about society and the media's contribution to our masculine identity, that's heavy, about how masculinity is killing us, killing me!'

Ex- partners and our ego

Another area that seems to be a regular talking point for some fathers and a topic that I discuss in other parts of my book is managing their relationships with their ex-partners. In particular, the negotiation around money, the buying of clothes and childcare seems to be a daily challenge. These relationships are usually historically complicated to decipher, mainly because we are not there, so it is difficult to pass judgement, but they can lead to heated, unresolved disagreements with ex-partners. This is why so many men I have met, once they have negotiated, talking openly in front of other men, were willing to talk about their experiences. There is no doubt that the older you get, the more you understand yourself and what makes your association with other people positive or negative. Therefore, some men can reflect on their turbulent pasts and start to understand the parts they played. You cannot change someone else, but you can try to change yourself. These men are striving to discard some of their negative masculine behaviours that can lead to fractious relationships with the following statements being made:

David: 'I'm stubborn, I know I am, and I just hate admitting I am wrong to anyone, much less my ex. I know, deep down, I need to back off and just admit I sometimes get it wrong, but I can't. I see backing down as a sign of weakness, so even when we were together after an argument, I want to tell my girl (partner) I'm sorry, and you are right, but it's hard. That's what I really want to work on my stubbornness because life is not always about who is right and wrong. It's about working things out without feeling you need to always be in charge and win the argument. I'm older (32 years old), and now I understand now where my stubbornness has come from. My mum always said that I took after my dad, but at the time, I didn't pay any attention. I guess I didn't really understand what she'd meant, but one day, after falling out with a good friend, I thought about my dad and people, family he had fallen out with over the years, and I realised that I was becoming like my dad and losing friends and partners because of my stubbornness. I couldn't continue thinking I was always right, even when I was wrong. That's part of the maleness I learned from my dad. Don't get me wrong. My dad was good in other areas, but I did learn that, as a male, I should know what's best and make a decision. The right decision. But now, I understand that my stance is placing lots of unnecessary pressure on my shoulders with things that should be cool, like seeing my two kids more often, and for what, my pride?'

Of course, not all fathers are willing to change. They are content with the way they are and feel that we are on a pointless journey of self-exploration. Again, it tended to be the older fathers, forty-plus, who have provided us with so many wise life experiences throughout the book, but like all of us, they eventually became set in their ways around certain aspects of their lives. As fathers pointed out:

Patterson: 'What is done is done, so why bother trying to change things now? The way I see it, men have always been masculine and women feminine. We hunted for food, and our woman looked after the children, and when we returned with our day's hunting, they would cook it. I love my wife. She is my world, but we understand our roles. I'm not saying it's perfect, but we blend together. You understand each other. The problem I see in the modern world is that everyone wants to do what everyone else does. Men want to be women, and women want to be men, and the balance is gone. That's what I see among the young and gender roles. We'll carry on until everyone is so confused, no one will know what he or she is doing. That's my opinion. I don't know if others see things the way I do. I'm not young anymore, so maybe everyone is cool with the mixed up... situation that is happening.'

Father: 'Conspiracy theory. We are what we are. We make choices about our lives. We are not puppets to be controlled. We need to take responsibility for our actions and not blame everyone else.'

Some fathers have questioned their effectiveness as fathers for a while and are ready to start new journeys and ways of thinking and behaving, with less of the arrogance, bravado, and suppression of their feelings for a more rounded, positive, and respectful approach to life and the people with whom they come into contact, more concerned about what we feel about ourselves and less concerned about what people think of them. This extends to all generations of fathers, so age is not particularly as significant as I thought it would be. This is reflected in this father's comment:

John: 'If I'm honest about my masculinity, there are things I have not liked about myself as a man for some time but didn't have anyone I felt would want to bounce my ideas off of. Apart from that, life is hectic, so finding the time was difficult, and I didn't really know how to start. I have to learn that giving my wife more does not mean I am less of a man. In fact, it means I am more of a man by letting go and not feeling I need to be the head of the house and make all the important decisions. My dad was in charge, but we are living in different times now. It's a joint thing; me and my wife are both in charge.'

We are not asking for masculinity to be destroyed, but we do want to kick start changes that will allow us to continue following healthier lifestyles for our families' sake and our own. We need to strike a balance between being masculine and positive activities associated with being a man: working hard and assisting in providing for our families, being responsible fathers and partners, showing and sharing our emotions, feelings, and fears with our wives, and making tough decisions within the family and community, and understanding that community is more important than individuals. In other words, the 'we' is more important than the 'I'.

This competition can be healthy, but not to the absolute detriment of others. Having feelings and sharing our emotions is healthier than keeping them in. To have regular relationships with our GPs or well-man clinics would mean accessing health care at earlier stages, averting life-threatening conditions such as prostrate cancer, eating balanced diets instead of rich foods as part of the culturally accepted masculine way of eating until our bellies are full. All of these areas have massive implications for us as individuals and to our children.

A wise woman named Sarah once told me that we are our children's televisions, and they watch and copy what we do, so if we transmit good programs, our children will learn good habits from us. I will make a bold statement to say that we need to spring clean our learned concepts of what masculinity means to us because these behaviours are not what it really means to be modern men in Britain.

I see this chapter not as a wake-up call as some have suggested, but as permission for us to explore topics we have not had the forum to do so in the past. All is not lost. Because we have the capacity to change, we do not have to accept every aspect of masculinity that has been laid out in front of us since birth.

A father's purpose in life

There is no getting away from it – part of the reason we are men on this earth is to be masculine, strong, protective, wise, loving, and caring towards our families and communities. Note the words 'caring' and 'loving', which are still viewed as feminine traits but are exactly what we need as well.

We are here to be with our wives or partners, not to live apart from them. We are here to bring up our children in a family unit, not to live apart from them. We are here to protect our families, not to expect the police to protect them from others and us. We are here to guide and discipline our sons and daughters, not expect teachers and other professionals to do so on our behalf. We are here to guide our communities and help our elders by knocking on their doors to make sure they are okay, doing odd jobs for them and not expect social services to do it all. We are here to defend, stand up, and at times, fight for the injustices to our communities, not leave it to lawyers and human rights activists. We are here to attend our children's parents' evenings and other social and school activities, not leave it for the mothers and grandparents to attend. We are here to financially support our families, not leave it to the benefits agency to provide them with poverty-level assistance. We are here to guide and protect our young sons from themselves and others who want to harm them, to protect, share, and guide our daughters who are intelligent, confident, and ambitious but face double standards due to their gender and race. We are here to embrace and understand formal education as a means of social mobility and role model a high work ethic by setting good examples for our children to follow and pass on to their children along with our family values. We are here to lead, support, and give hope to our families and partners by not running away from our responsibilities as they have spent centuries trying to keep our family and community units together.

As one father has said, the list is quite daunting. I agree, so see it as a work in progress by seeing the areas you feel you can work on without feeling you need to do it all because most of us mere mortals cannot. But it is clear from meeting the fathers that these areas, which are not exhaustive, is partly what being a man is really about – standing up to your responsibilities because if you do not look after your families and your wider communities, who will? This is why some of our women are so vexed with us. They can see how some of us are either unwilling or unable to do our duties towards our families and communities. Irrelevant of whether your relationship with your partner has ended acrimoniously or not, we are still fathers with responsibilities that do not end if we do not live with our families. Primary school children still need you to attend their assemblies. Teenagers still need assistance to buy books, class equipment, clothes, and boundary-setting to back up mum's rules. Also, no matter what their age, children still need time to talk with Dad. Your emotional and financial assistance does not end because you are estranged from your ex-partner; it carries on until your children grow and are able to stand on their own two feet. This is the deal we entered when having children. This is how real men gain respect from the wider society, our sisters, and our children. As one father explained earlier, it's a bit hard to respect his dad because he did not provide for him and his sister, especially when he remembers the times he went to bed hungry.

Masculinity is a lifelong, constructed behaviour that you cannot just throw away like a toy. It is embedded in our minds by intricate control structures I have spoken about in this chapter that exist all around us from birth through to death. I'm happy to say that some fathers I met are already trying to readdress the imbalance with their sons. One father who earlier explained that his father had told him he was too old for a hug, realised that he was becoming like his dad, having a moan at his son just like his father had done to him as a boy and becoming emotionally distant and detached:

> **Mohammed:** 'I could see my father in me, and I didn't like what I saw, so I flung my arms around my son and told him I loved him, and he said the same back to me. I've been through so much in life, but that was one of the hardest and emotional things I have ever done with my son. I felt like I had broken the family curse. Now, it is up to me to carry on, showing I care. I can't go back now, and I don't want to go back, just forward.'

It was very emotional listening to his and other fathers' stories about how they were fighting back against their upbringing, allowing their emotions that had been curtailed as boys to resurface and repair the generational damage between the fathers and sons in their families. I think this father will be okay because he has taken steps to dispel the myth of masculinity 'boxing him in'. This father, in his own way, realised that the pressure of gender stress – the need to show how masculine you are so you do not disappoint others – was killing his relationship with his son. Masculinity controlled this father for so long that he decided he would break free and not allow it to control him.

> **Terrance:** 'My life revolves around my family and church. We are very busy doing projects for our church. All my children are involved with our church, and so is my extended family. I do not know another life, but some of the things I am hearing seem a bit selfish; that number one is important above all else. You cannot let yourself just be selfish and just look out for yourself in life because you will

not learn that others have needs, too. That is not right. You have to put God at the centre of everything you do; otherwise, where will you find the answers to life's dilemmas? I think that you should let God guide you as I have seen too many men lose their way by being selfish and stubborn in life and having no friends or family to help them in their times of need.'

Nowhere in my earlier definitions of masculinity will you find the mention of responsibility or duty to your family or community. Why? Because advertisers do not really care about your family or community responsibilities compared to the products they want to sell and the images or fantasies of masculinity, they need to perpetuate in order to sell their products to you.

Behind every great man is

It is no coincidence that the long-held view is that behind every great man is a great woman. Time and time again, I heard the enormous praise and utter love and devotion towards partners, wives, mothers, grandmothers, and aunts for their unwavering love, encouragement, and support throughout the years. Fathers continue to praise their partners because they know their guidance and listening ear assists them to make the right choices in life, and their unconditional love and support even through the dark times are what has brought them to where they are now. This is partly based on the traditional African and Caribbean model of support, whereby the women stood side by side with their men, even in battle, before gender programming dealt us different roles. In modern-day Britain, there is no denying that we live in a world where males dominate the most powerful positions in life. Some of us can, at times, forget our partners' support networks with their wealth of contacts, information, and support into which they can tap when help is needed. Let me give you an example:

Simon: 'I can be difficult at times. Our fridge broke down, and I tried to fix it but couldn't. My partner told me she knew a few people that could fix the fridge, but I assumed it would cost a lot, you know how high call out fees are... on top of the parts and labour. I finally had to give in. Our food was going off, so she called one of her girlfriends, who called this guy. He came round within two hours, no call out fee, just the cost of parts and labour. I'm telling you; my wife has this intricate network that seems to know someone for every conceivable job known to man, but I don't like asking for help because I feel I should be able to do these things myself, but sometimes, I just need to allow my wife a little slack and allow her to help me out a bit and work her magic.'

So, we thank you.

Mirror, Mirror on the Wall:
The Father-Daughter Relationship

"My mission in life is not to merely survive, but to thrive; and to do so with some passion, some compassion, some humour and some style."
– Maya Angelou

Daddy's girl

A father-daughter relationship is probably one of the most fascinating and complex ones you will experience as a father. Why? Because our frames of reference are not first-hand experiences of being a woman in a society where, although women have taken massive steps in education and the workplace, gender roles still define their life's chances and opportunities. Unlike yours.

Also, there is an expectation that, as a male and father, you will be close and protect your daughter from all dangers until the day comes that she is able to protect herself. Our personal attitudes and upbringings towards gender are likely to define our parenting approaches where our daughters are concerned, and this is the challenge fathers face in modern day Britain. Our attitudes and own upbringings may bring out a more traditional approach towards our daughters' upbringings than we thought, compared to our sons. In contrast, some fathers may have a more modern approach whereby they are much more involved with their daughters' upbringings than their fathers ever were.

As a part of our protective role towards our daughters, there exists terminology in society that defines and reinforces what our fatherly duties should be. When my daughter was around four years old, the first terminology I came across was 'daddy's girl', and 'she has you wrapped around her little finger'. These terms – from both men and women – confirmed the expectation that I should be close to my daughter. I remember meeting a dear friend in a shopping centre who hanged with my daughter and me for a while. She observed our relationship and commented, 'Aaliyah has you wrapped around her little finger!' I challenged my friend by stating that my daughter was only a four-year-old child and not capable of such deception. My friend asked me to look at my daughter's hand and tell him what I saw. My daughter was happily licking the ice cream I had previously said she could not have! I realised then and there that if 'wrapping me around her little finger' meant getting her own way, well, Aaliyah had won, hands down. The thing is, I really do not remember how she persuaded me to buy the ice cream for her. My friends like to remind me that it was the look of Aaliyah's puppy dog eyes and lowered voice tone that had done the trick. She had such wonderful big eyes – how could I possibly say no to her? Whatever she had done to get me to buy her the ice cream, it had worked, and there highlights the dynamics in father-daughter relationships.

There is something emotionally special about having a daughter that can melt the heart of even the most hardened of men. I have witnessed men who were known to be fearless melt to their daughter's wishes. It certainly was a golden period for me as it enabled me to escape the competitive and unforgiving world of work to show emotion and love towards my daughter. My daughter, Aaliyah, helped me to keep a work-life balance, detracting me from the routine of the rat race in which we live, and I thank her for that.

We are forever trying to understand the female world because our frames of reference as men are so different from that of our daughters. In fact, a lot of men have spent most of their lives running away from anything associated with their feminine sides, and then, along came our daughters to remind us that about which we feel uncomfortable.

As they grow, terminology, such as 'daddy's girl', starts to fade, and the 'girl power' of the 12- to 16-year-old kicks in, and they are full of intelligence, opinions, attitude, the ability to express themselves, inquisitiveness, and an abundance of confidence. She is no longer that little four-year-old girl who enticed me to buy her that ice cream. She no longer wants to spend time with only you, as her friends are more interesting to be with. After all, they have similar interests, and together, they become immersed in their teenage world. I remember finding myself in a mild form of mourning over the partial loss of my daughter's time being transferred to her friends, but I was consoled by the fact this was healthy, natural, and a part of the process of her growing up. That is, until one day when we realise that we have grown apart and some aspects of her teenage world are just irritating! You are more than happy to escape from the fashion, music, and celebrity worlds and girl crushes that seem to change every month. She lives and breathes this world that has absolutely no importance to me. After all, it's all very superficial when compared to music from my era, when the words in songs were more important than the style. In doing so, we start to lose our connections with our daughters in ways that are not immediately obvious but will become clear as they continue to mature.

I hear time and time again, from fathers that are far from being close to their teenage daughters that an ongoing tension exists. Both sides complain of the other, not understanding where they are coming from, and some cannot even remember when and why the feud began. Whatever happened to the closeness between the little girl of whom he was proud when people called her 'daddy's girl'? Some fathers admit to becoming fearful of their daughters being too open and expressive and at times, over the top where emotions or 'drama', as some fathers have described it, are concerned, so we distance ourselves, believing that Mum should exclusively deal with this juncture in our daughters lives because we feel uncomfortable. Other fathers have explained that they became angry with their daughters' being secretive, which means she must be up to no good, so their responses were to control their movements. I will explain later in this chapter why it is so important to stay emotionally in contact with our daughters' worlds as they grow and mature.

You're a man, so you're part of the problem!

There are so many gender challenges our daughters will need to negotiate as they grow older, and keeping up as fathers can be difficult but absolutely necessary if you value having good relationships with your daughters in the future. So, as fathers, rather than run miles from their worlds, we need to be prepared for the journeys ahead. As our daughters become older, new sets of challenges will test their resolve and yours. The sad truth is that as men you are a symptom, a part of the bigger gender challenges she will experience throughout her life at work and at home. The fact is that no matter how far women have progressed, historically, men control society, and to a large extent, have tried to control women through society's structures. Let me give you some examples.

There are many cultures that value males born more than females born, and this is shown by the way they treat the two. Boys are allowed to play, and girls are expected to help with the home chores. Girls are expected to be responsible, whereas boys are allowed to be carefree and reckless. Boys are allowed to bring their girlfriends to their bedrooms, and girls are not. Boys are allowed – and even encouraged by some fathers' own behaviours towards women – to have more than one girlfriend, and I hear fathers saying, 'That's my boy,' but if their daughters do the same thing, it is treated with disdain. Boys are encouraged to sow their wild oats, whereas girls are forever warned to control their sexual desires as pregnancy can be the consequence. Boys are allowed to stay out longer than their sisters, and in the main, their whereabouts is not challenged by their parents. Boys are not expected to cook (unless they live in a household where Dad does), and why should they? Dad does not lift a finger, so the daughters help the mums. I could go on, but I think you get the message. I haven't even spoken about what happens to women in the world of school, fashion, diet, work, relationships, and health where, already, you can see how your daughter's life is controlled by men...by you.

We are talking about sexism and power but within families, children's attitudes are moulded and accepted as normal. So, your gender is very much a part of either the problem or the solution your daughter will face throughout her life, because how you treat your daughter and the other women in your family will help her formalise how she expects to be treated in her relationships and in the wider society. Our experiences as males and fathers can help shape our daughters' attitudes, behaviours, and frames of reference for how she expects to be treated as a woman by others, including her future husband/wife or boss. Help her through the maze of sexism so you can place her in an advantageous position rather than that of a victim.

The world of beauty, fashion, and diet

This seems like a good starting place if we want to keep pace with understanding and being involved in your daughters' worlds. There is a minefield of information and advertising within the beauty, fashion, and dietary industries, attempting to shape our daughters' minds as to how they should look and what they should wear. In addition, there are both traditional and post-modern female theorists battling it out as to how women should be defined. Simplistically put, this determines whether women should stay at home and look after their children or have the right to careers and enter the world of work. If you have struggled as I have at times to understand what shapes our daughters' perceptions of who they are, this chapter is probably a good starting point.

Of course, the family plays a major role in our daughters' self-esteem, but in modern-day Britain, social media and advertising wield a lot of influence in so many areas of our lives. The multi-billion-dollar industries of fashion, beauty, and diet seem to be the areas that confuse us dads the most and influence our daughters' day-to-day lives the most. It seems that young girls and women are forever being informed of how they should look, what they should wear, how to be sexy, the ideal weight for women, what they should eat (or not eat) to stay slim and healthy, and the new, must-try diets in town. For older women, the beauty industry has cleverly marketed anti-winkle creams, proclaiming to slow the ageing process.

Girl-guiding UK questioned 1,109 young girls and women aged seven to 21 years old about their attitudes towards life. Half of the girls across Britain admit they would consider a 'nip and tuck' to enhance their appearances, and 27% want to be thinner. The report highlighted that the main contributing factor for girls feeling this way is the bombardment of images of airbrushed celebrities and the growing popularity of cosmetic surgery that places a lot of pressure on children. Of course, men and women are their own agents of choice, and you do not need me to break down these industries' complex motivations to entice us to buy their products or whether their claims of being a 'better you' are true. I am far from being an expert to pass judgement, but what is clear to me is that the targeting of products for both men and women starts at an early age and continues into old age.

Not surprisingly, then, in modern Britain, there is a preoccupation with being slim and attractive. Body image, it would seem for girls, women, and men, is of the utmost importance and seems to outweigh a person's IQ or character. For some, especially the young, the clothes they wear make a bigger statement than the qualifications they have. Also, your body shape and whether you are considered beautiful can determine how people perceive and treat you, and most importantly, how you perceive yourself. Women should not be defined by looks alone, but the sad fact is that so many industries – such as fitness, music, fashion, and the celebrity circuit, to name a few – are driven by this very concept. A part of the message to women seems to be that they need their products because without it, they are just, well...ordinary, irrelevant.

These are the kinds of messages with which our daughters must contend every day as they try to develop and define their identities. Whether you are a man or a woman, we should acknowledge that all these industries have their uses and can play important roles in our lives, and the newest cosmetics on the market can make us feel good about ourselves.

I do not want you to get the impression that boys and men are immune from the pressures of body shape and image as they are not. The pressure on boys is to have a masculine body, and the main, modern-day pressure is to exhibit an abdominal six-pack. Boys' and men's magazines show masculine models and storylines to which boys are meant to aspire to. Along with this image are many traits, some destructive, that boys are expected to develop to be seen as masculine and emotionless. I talk about this at length in the chapter called **From Boyhood to Manhood** and how, as fathers, we can challenge some of these negative traits aimed at our sons.

Whatever the age of your daughter, she is already being bombarded with information overload about how she should look and the added pressure of the European definition of 'beauty'. Feelings of not fitting into the narrow definitions of beauty or body shape can, at times, irritate and upset girls. Trying to grapple with liking what she sees in the mirror every morning – her hair, complexion, body, legs, or nose – can be difficult at times, for young, Black girls in particular, who may not identify with the majority of models, celebrities, pop stars, or actresses they see every day on their laptops, tablets, or mobiles and in online magazines.

It is not that our daughters go around with their heads down, thinking about their appearances every minute of the day, far from it. Nowadays, there are many more positive Black female images – such as Beyoncé, Alexandra Burke, Maya Jama, Clara Amfo or Rihanna (a representation of light and dark skin complexions) – with whom they can identify and aspire to be like and look like in fashion and cosmetics. Also, I cannot stress enough the vital role played by family members with positive mums, young aunties, and grandparents who help build their strong characters and self-esteems, but online magazines and advertisements send out very powerful images and messages to all our daughters around the country, regardless colour. Showing what is considered the 'perfect' or 'ideal' woman can, at times, place doubt within our daughters' minds. The saying that 'the mirror does not lie' can be a powerful feedback loop to what they really think about what they see in the mirror. Because they do not resemble these models or celebrities on the fronts of magazines, on catwalks, or the majority of actresses on TV, is it any wonder that some start to question their looks or parts of their body?

So, what does this have to do with us fathers, you may ask, and what can fathers possibly do to assist their daughters in this dilemma? Isn't this the stuff that mothers talk to their daughters about, and we should stay well clear of it all, I hear you say? The answer is, yes, mothers are integral parts of our daughters' lives, but that should not negate the parts we play. The simple truth is that we cannot prevent the various industries from targeting and communicating with our daughters or our sons, for that matter, unless we move our families to deserted islands. But, as one father said, 'We can contribute to how our daughters see themselves by keeping their confidences intact.'

The reason why we as fathers have important parts to play is that times have changed with the increase in the amount of leisure time we spend with our children. So, our daughters may feel quite comfortable asking us questions that our sisters would never have asked our fathers as their relationships are so different. Our fathers had to work long hours to make ends meet, so there was little time for father-daughter relationships to flourish. So, our attentiveness and conversations with our daughters will matter to them, as we are the first representatives of the male species in their lives, so we need to be both thoughtful and prepared to ensure we do not crush their confidences.

Questions such as, 'Dad, what do you think of my hair?' or 'Do you think my bum or thighs are too fat?' are two common questions fathers have informed they have dealt with. Times have really changed as I know my sisters would never have dreamed of asking our dad such questions. The traditional type of fathers who have kept out of the so-called 'women's issues' are still around. I know – I have met them on my journey – and we should not judge them too harshly because they choose not to get involved. Not all men feel comfortable or able to get involved as they may do more damage than good, so a judgement call will need to be made, but there are techniques that even the most unconfident father can learn that I will talk about later in the chapter.

The supermarket and newsagent test

Whilst shopping at the supermarket and newsagent, some of the fathers look at the magazine stands so they can get a sense of the fashion and beauty industries' messages to their daughters. They want to try to see through their daughters' eyes the types of teen magazines on sale on the stands. The fathers were surprised by their findings. A reoccurring comment among the fathers was that they had previously not noticed just how many female magazines were on offer. Some fathers admitted to regularly buying or browsing through their computer or car magazines, but it was not until they consciously took a step back that they realised the sheer numbers of magazines with advice on relationships, hair care, fashion, make-up, sex, and dieting, to name a few.

> **Jeff:** 'You know what? I was shocked, shocked by what I saw. Have you looked in a teen magazine before? I don't know if the one I picked up represented all of them, but most of the pages were about celebrities acting badly, who's going out with whom and diets, diets, and more diets. I didn't really realise or think about what my daughter is reading and how this must affect her.'

Steve: 'The magazine I looked at was okay, more balanced. There were humorous captions taking the mickey out of celebrities and advice from celebrities on the type of bikini to wear depending on your body shape. I could see my daughter finding that article informative. What I would say is the pressure on female celebrities to look good all the time was really obvious. If they didn't look good, the offending picture was followed by bitchy comments, and that seems to be the norm. I looked at the reporters' names, and they were all females. I suppose the saying that women dress for other women and not their men must be true.'

Even more alarming for the fathers was the lack of Black representation adorning the fronts and insides of these magazines. One father summed up what a few fathers were saying: 'I was pushed to find two or three Black models on the front covers of approximately 40 magazines, then I realised the limited choice my daughter had to find someone that looked like her.' Another father said, 'I was surprised at the pictures and messages to teenage girls, the preoccupation with finding a boyfriend and romance, and the adult clothes they are being encouraged to wear.'

Under-representation of women of colour

The magazines, whether innocently or purposely, do not represent or promote women of colour in the fashion or beauty industries. Of course, there are a few British and American-based Black magazines that work very hard at representing girls and women. They need to be applauded, but what of the other magazines' representation, considering we live in a multicultural country?

The message to our daughters from the majority of these magazines is a gesture when it comes to them mattering, but only in a narrow and limiting way. That is, if they fit a size 4 with no shape and look as if they have anorexia. This is why our daughters tend to focus on fashion, beauty ideas, and the identities of American female R&B and/or hip-hop artists, American film stars, or in the business world, due to the limited magazines on offer in Britain.

Talking to my sisters and female friends, the lack of Black representation was even more acute 20 to 30 years ago, and they had limited role models who were viewed as beautiful and no global communication like the Internet that could bring this information to their doorsteps to counter the negative image of dark-skinned girls and women. Therefore, for some, but not for all, their confidence as dark-skinned girls could, at times, be low, and this was reinforced by taunts at school. There were few works of literature, magazines, singing artists, and/or actresses to which to aspire. In turn, some girls found it difficult to believe they were beautiful in the true sense of the word. These women of the '70s and '80s feel very differently about themselves today. A part of this change is the perception of what is now considered beautiful and improved representation with the inception of satellite TV and social media. These women have made such huge political, social, employment, and financial strides over the last 20 years. My sisters and female friends, all mothers today, were pivotal in the battle for Black women to be acknowledged as beautiful, and they paved the way for their daughters to feel much more comfortable about their beauty. Ironically, although outside of this books remit. Fathers are aware of the cultural momentum towards the pursuit of some White women using cosmetic surgery in their desire to have fuller figures that resemble women of colour.

When talking about our daughters, one of the fatherhood groups came to realise our unconditional love and natural desires to protect our daughters from harm. However, what was missing was our understanding of how important identity is to their existence, growing up as young women of colour, where their types of African and Caribbean beauty and physique were not directly celebrated or pushed as natural and the pressures and challenges this entails for them.

A pledge to our daughters

Armed with their supermarket and newsagent test experiences, our discussions focused on the pressure from the fashion, beauty, and diet industries who target their marketing machines towards our daughters; our lack of emotional connection to their world, especially in the teenage years; how our daughters feel about their images and looks; the sexism perpetrated by us within our homes and in the world of work; and our roles in consolidating women's positions in society, which left some fathers much more aware of the world in which their daughters have to live.

> **Paul:** 'I used to be really close to my daughter, but as she got older, she seemed to have gone another way from me. When I think about it, what she did was natural. I guess, as a teenage girl, she became interested in fashion, college friends, and college subjects that have moved on since my time at college. We grew apart and had less in common. I didn't give up on being close to her as she still needed financing, but I felt more like her bank manager, either agreeing or disagreeing on her spending. So, she was either happy or vexed with me – there was no in-between. When I think about the amount of time we used to spend together and now – what a difference! The various topics discussed earlier made me think about how I can try to understand my daughter's world and take more of an interest in some areas she enjoys. I know I can't bring back the past and make her a little girl again, but at least I can try to communicate with her a little more.'

A lot of the fathers I met were willing, but they struggled to find solutions though they were open and ready to becoming more involved in their daughters' lives, as well as providing them with more protection and cautionary words of advice to back up their partners' quests for their daughters to strive for excellence, how they expected to be treated by boys and the wider public, and how they felt about themselves because they were beautiful from the inside and on the outside. What our daughters saw every morning when they looked into the mirror was a good starting point and an indicator of what they really felt about themselves on any given day. Teaching our children to love themselves forms the basis for having positive self-esteem and our acceptance to change our sexist attitudes and behaviour within the home

The 'positive mirror reflection' and how to use it

Like it or not, fathers, our roles in our daughters' lives can, at times, influence how they feel and what they perceive of themselves when they look in the mirror. The 'positive mirror reflection' is an aid for helping you and your daughter to broach subjects that can be difficult to talk about or to find an opening to talk about them. I have met fathers who find it difficult to verbalise their love and appreciation towards their daughters. As one father explained, 'Sometimes, I just want to tell her I love her and say how proud I am of her, but the words won't come out of my mouth. I feel uncomfortable, so I don't say it, although I know I should.' The roots of our emotional blocks come from our parents, who were not hot on words of encouragement or openly showing their emotions. A stern word or a cuss would never stop them from making sure you were never hungry; that was their way of showing they cared. Of course, we were far too young to understand the intricacies of their Morse code language and behaviour. We just knew to be careful of what we said and how we behaved around adults.

Later on in life, we can now understand the subtle messages of caring and encouragement that was being passed on through food.

I was also made aware by the fathers that not all parents tried to communicate positive messages of encouragement, and a cuss was just, well, a cuss. So, here lies the difficulty for fathers. If we did not receive open emotion or appreciation from our parents, how are we able to reciprocate this with our daughters? Hopefully, the 'positive mirror reflection' method will give us a vehicle to express our feelings to our daughters.

I do not take total credit for this concept, although we did come up with the name. I had a long discussion with a close female friend, and she spoke of the importance of what her daughters see whilst looking in the mirror and how this had an impact on their moods and confidence. She spoke about the importance of fathers positively acknowledging their daughters' looks and personalities and not just leaving it to the mothers. During a discussion in one of the fathers' groups I attended, I asked whether we could use the 'positive mirror reflection' concept to aid us to communicate with our daughters. This started our education on how we could consciously build a platform for discussion with our daughters by using an item they learnt to use early on in life on a day-to-day basis: the mirror.

Girls and women throughout history and across cultures have a unique relationship with mirrors. I must say at this juncture that men also have an inquisitive relationship with mirrors in their teenage years, surrounding their growing facial hair, muscles and penis size, so this is not exclusive to girls.

The mirror provides a historical and present medium for both men and women. Our daughters cognitively process a feedback loop on how they look based on their reflections, and the information gained is either positively or negatively processed. This processed information can, at times, dictate how a girl or woman feels about their looks or body on a given day, and ultimately, what action she is willing to take to improve what she sees. As the saying goes, the mirror never lies. Some girls diet and exercise, and some accept the way they are and get on with life. If your daughter looks in the mirror and is content with what she sees, you are fortunate, as even supermodels are known to find faults. Also, this does not mean that because she feels disheartened one day, she will feel the same the next day. That's where, as a father, using the 'positive mirror reflection' can be a useful tool to assist you in improving your emotional connection and communication avenues with your daughter.

I'm sure that, in passing, you see your daughter using a mirror in the home as you pass by and think nothing of it; it's just a normal, everyday situation, so you leave her to her own devices. Once in a while, try stopping and standing at the mirror with your daughter and

- ask her about what she sees when she looks in the mirror – be ready for both positive and negative comments;
- talk positively to her about what you see in basic terms, the changes in her hair, her big bright smile, or even her nose – you choose;
- talk to her about which parts she has inherited from her favourite aunts or grandparents, so she understands that others in the family have similar traits, and she is not alone;
- communicate to your daughter the good things you see and give your interpretation of how the outside world sees her personality and character;
- communicate and acknowledge her appearance and that how she feels is important to you;
- transmit to her the notion that although you are busy, you still have time to spend with her and talk to her because you care; and

- Note that there are no bigger gifts you can give to your daughter than to tell her that she is beautiful or smart and showing that you care by giving her big hugs.

Fathers testing the waters

A few fathers shared with me their experiences of taking the chance opportunities to use the 'positive mirror reflection' with their daughters.

One father explained that his family was getting ready to go out, and his wife had finished their 12-year-old daughter's hair, and everything seemed okay. The father was much more aware of his daughter's mood, her behaviour during this process, than he had ever been before. Usually, he worried about finding his car, making sure he had his wallet, and getting everyone out of the house, which was usually quite a feat, but not on that day. His daughter was irritated by something he initially sensed and then saw by her body language and facial expressions. He allowed his eyes to pursue her movements and moods rather than be preoccupied with the usual distractions or irritation of her taking too long to get ready. As they walked to their car, he noticed that his daughter had stopped at another car and was checking her hair and fidgeting with it in the car's wing mirror. The father asked his daughter if everything was okay. His daughter, not used to Dad stopping and asking her such a question, hesitated for a moment and said she was unsure about her hairstyle and didn't want her friends to criticise her hair. Ordinarily, he would not comment because he would be preoccupied with other thoughts and would not be emotionally attuned to showing an interest in his daughter's thoughts or actions, but he stopped and asked her what she felt was wrong with her hairstyle. His daughter said that one of the plaits was at an odd angle, and this was making her feel silly. She did not want other people to see her hair sticking up like that.

The father helped his daughter realign the plait and explained to her how beautiful her hair looked. His daughter was taken aback by her father's comments and said, 'Do you really think so because I was unsure?' The father said, 'Yes. I have always liked that hairstyle on you. It reminds me of the Caribbean girls going to school with their plaits and ribbons in their hair.' His daughter was so happy with her father's affirmation of her and her hair that her whole mood was lifted for the day.

The whole scenario took approximately two minutes, but within that time, the father had acknowledged his daughter's thoughts and actions. The dialogue between him and his daughter had been uplifting, and he commented that for those few minutes, he felt emotionally and spiritually connected to his daughter, more than he had since she was a young girl.

Tyson: 'That was a scary moment talking to my daughter as she fidgeted with her hair in the car's wing mirror because I didn't really know what I was doing. I just played it by ear and tried to say the right things. That bothered me more than if I had said something that was insensitive; I can do that at times. I don't know, but it seemed to click, and our conversation was a nice kind of special. I have wanted to say things like that to her before, but I never knew when the right time was or what to say. I hope we can have more conversations, not just about her hair, but about other things she is thinking about.'

Hopefully, your daughter will start to feel more comfortable with you if you show more of an interest in the teenage world you have previously tried to avoid, and maybe, just maybe, she will not just seek out her mum all the time.

Surprises in store
A common feature of young teenage girls of colour – but certainly not exclusive to them – is their dislike of certain parts of their bodies because

they believe it to be too big, or too small, or too short, or too long. For instance, an African father said that his daughter did not like her bottom because she believed it was too big. The father reminded her that Serena Williams had won the Australian Tennis Open and made the point that, though the media had criticised her for being overweight, unfit, and said that her bottom was too big to win the tournament, her large bum had not been a hindrance to her success.

Also, Hollywood is obsessed with Beyoncé and Jennifer Lopez's rear end to the point where you can now buy underwear that enhances your bottom to look bigger, so what is the message to women? Bottom aside, it is fantastic that his daughter felt she had an open enough relationship with her father to include him in such a discussion. Of course, their relationship did not happen overnight. Her parents had nurtured their relationship, allowing her the space to feel able to talk to them. They, in return, were able to put her concerns into perspective and at the same time, allow her to see that having a large bum can be an asset rather than a hindrance. His wife and her aunts had also inherited the physical gene, so she had adults she could talk to who would be sensitive and have the same experiences.

Although all of 'daddy's little girls' eventually grow up, Paul and Tyson's comments show us how we can still reach our daughters, given the right circumstances. However, a word of caution: if we are not careful, communication can become problematic if all we do is criticise or shout at our daughters or any child, for that matter. Hence the importance of talking about what is going on in their lives in a non-judgemental way. Otherwise, you run the risk of your children deciding not to tell you anything because they know your reaction will be to hit the roof with anger. Of course, understanding your daughter's world is not just about the mirror, as she will have a full social life, and her interests will be varied, including things such as fashion, films, music, boys, career guidance, peer groups, and education so she will not be permanently glued to the mirror. So, the mirror is just one method to kick start communication to ensure we can go into their worlds and show them you are still interested in their lives, the actual topic. Like Paul, the father, said, once you feel more comfortable, you will be able to discuss other topics with your daughter without needing the mirror as a tool for introducing discussion.

Now, you may be thinking one of two things. Either whatever it takes to have some form of connection and be closer to my daughter, I will give it a go, or this is just not for me; I prefer to leave these types of issues to her mother. It's your choice, really, as I understand that not all fathers are cut out for this type of close association with their daughters. Interestingly, I did find many fathers who felt they did not want to improve their communication with their daughters. The sticking point seems to be whether they had the courage to do something about it.

> **Kemi:** 'My wife and her aunts are formidable people with strong characters and a lot of life experience. Even if I wanted to it's better... our roles are already set, and they are doing a good job, so I do not feel the need to change anything.'

The man in the mirror: who will your daughter end up dating?
If you do decide that you want to use the 'positive mirror reflection' as an introduction to talk to your daughter, be aware that the mirror also includes another person: you. If you are standing in the mirror with your daughter and talking about her, your presence in the mirror is also there. What you see is what your daughter sees every day, her father, and how he conducts himself. How do you communicate and relate to others? Do you swear when under pressure or try to remain calm and work things out by problem-solving? Do you treat your partner and/or wife with respect or take her for granted? Are you a moaner or a problem solver? Do you cook, clean, or iron or leave it all to your partner and children? Do you smoke or

drink heavily or in moderation? Do you prefer to be out with the boys or try to provide a healthy balance between your friends and family time? Does your family know your friends, or do you keep them separate?

The list is endless, so we will stop there. The point we are trying to make is that you can have a direct effect on how your daughter views you and the types of relationships your daughter will have later in life. If you treat her with respect, accept her without condition for the person she is, and not limit or control her with the gender double standards that exist when compared to her brothers, it is likely that she will grow up with a positive concept of herself. In turn, she will expect her future partners, work colleagues, and friends to treat her how dad does, and she will be unlikely to accept a person that is the opposite of you. However, if you are a male chauvinist, look down on women, and expect everything to be done around the home for you because you are the king of your castle, don't be upset if she ends up with someone like you and complains that her life is a misery. After all, you were her yardstick in judging men!

A part of our responsibility towards our daughters as their main male influence is to conduct ourselves in a gender conscious manner. Of course, we are not saints, and as human beings, we will make mistakes in life. Some members in the group decided (not all of the group, after all, this was a democracy) that they could learn from their past mistakes and try to be conscious about some of the language and negative behaviours their daughters sometimes witnessed within the home. Although these men wanted to remain anonymous, I commend them for trying to change their ways and make a new start as better role models for their daughters.

Positive strokes

'Positive strokes' is an area with which some – but not all – fathers were familiar and about which they were able to talk. Some were consistent when communicating this to their children whilst others admitted they could do more. Some of the fathers set themselves homework (this caused a lot of laughter in some groups who thought their homework days had ended a long time ago): for one month, they would try to say positive things to their daughters rather than moan or be preoccupied with work, DIY, or paying bills. They would then give feedback to the group as to how it had gone.

Some fathers enthusiastically embraced their tasks, while others struggled to find time from their normal routines. Some of the older fathers did not want to participate in the homework task, as 'positive strokes' was not something they felt comfortable doing with their children on a consistent basis. They came from the school of hard knocks in which they were programmed to be tough and not worry about self-doubt or what the world thought about them. They believed there was too much emphasis placed on psychological child-centred methods, and people needed to accept who they were and get on with life. The old sticks and stones may break my bones adage is alive and kicking within these fathers, so you can guess that they also thought the 'positive mirror reflection' approach an exercise in self-indulgence.

So, into which camp do you fit? Here are a few positive strokes ideas the group came up with through trial and error with their daughters. All have had some level of success with the fathers to whom I have spoken, while others refuse to use them for the previously given reasons.

1. Think of a special name for your daughter (i.e., princess, doctor, sweet pea, or something else) that holds a special meaning for you. The special name will not replace her birth name, but it will be used at times when you feel the need to communicate warmth or acknowledge your daughter. Yours and her understanding of the word show the special relationship you have with her and that you care to the extent that you have a special name for her. There was

a word of warning from a father who informed us how well his special name had been going with his daughter until he'd embarrassed her by using it in front of her friends. If you are going to use a special name your daughter finds slightly embarrassing but does not mind you using it in private, keep the name private, just within the family.

2. I remember reading a book on how to become rich, and the author spoke about the importance of finding time from his extremely busy schedule to spend with his daughter. This was surprising at the time, as family never gets a mention in the high-powered world of corporate America. This highly successful man had developed 'special days' he spent with his daughter. As his daughter got older, he found that her tastes had become more mature, and visits to the zoo had been replaced with visits to the museum or cinema. He also spoke about his daughter's transformation from being a student to becoming the educator in their relationship. At a museum they visited, she explained the purpose of certain brush strokes in a painting or a complicated storyline he could not follow in a film they had watched at the cinema. He did not have to pretend to know everything, as they shared their thoughts and experiences. I always thought this was a great story – no matter how busy you are, you should find time, special time, to spend with your daughter. This time together is priceless, and it can help you build an everlasting bond with your daughter long after she decides she wants to hang out with her girlfriends or boyfriend instead.

3. Let your daughter know when she does something thoughtful, helps someone, thinks of a good idea, scores well in a test, or recited her times table. 'I really like the way you...' It's totally up to you to decide what thoughtful action she has done to fill the gap in the quotation, but you are communicating to her pride in the way she had handled

something, and this praise will help her know that you notice her and value her input.

4. I know the fast pace of modern living is making family dinner a rarity. However, it is a good place to ask both girls and boys about their days at school, college, work, or university. It shows them that as a family unit, you can talk, listen to each other, and take an interest in their lives.

5. The 'positive mirror reflection'. See earlier parts of this chapter.

6. Write notes to your daughter or any child in the family who has achieved something at school, college, within the family, or community, explaining how proud you are of them. This idea has proven successful with the older dads in the group as another form of expression rather than verbal affirmation, which made them feel uncomfortable. You could also allow your children to use notes to write about something that has upset them as a way to start the discussion. Of course, you will need to approach them to verbally finish the conversation, otherwise, you could be up writing to each other all night.

Getting past our uncomfortable feelings: talking to our daughters

If we are going to try to connect with our daughters like during the 'daddy's girl' era, we need to deal with the sticky stuff in which we would probably just prefer not to get involved. This 'sticky stuff' with which fathers seem to feel uncomfortable about in no particular order are:

1) the constant talking and drama with friends,
2) puberty,
3) sex and pregnancy, and

4) the thorny topic of boys and what constitutes a healthy relationship

The drama: Some fathers are concerned that if they open up and talk to their daughters more often, the gates will burst open, and they may hear and have to deal with stuff of which they are not capable. However, the by-product of this 'stand back approach' is that we end up feeling, at times, distant from our daughters' worlds and unable to salvage a meaningful relationship.

> **Clint**: 'My 15-year-old daughter is filled with school drama, and it makes me uncomfortable. I backed off when she started secondary school. The graphic details of her arguments or issues with her friends started and it drained me. Secondary school relationships are much more complicated than in primary school. I left these things to her mother, who seems to handle it better and has...ideas much better than me.'

Such comments were typical but not exclusive to all the fathers I met. However, those fathers who spoke about using their partners as mediums of communication found that, although they had good communication with their daughters, talking to their daughters about personal issues had gradually decreased over the years. In turn, their daughters ended up feeling they could not talk to their fathers about personal and relationship issues. In my introduction, I mentioned that we had been very close to our daughters during the 'daddy's girl' period in which there was nothing we could not fix or talk about in relation to primary school and we were their supermen. However, as time went by and our daughters got older, they realised that we were fallible, with good and bad points. It may sound obvious, but a pattern I found among fathers is an acceptance that fixing a broken toy was a lot easier than fixing their daughters' friendships.

Giving advice on a range of interpersonal issues does not come easily to a lot of fathers because their experiences and relationships as young boys were completely different when compared to their daughters.

> **Eric:** 'I haven't got the answers when she tells me that one of her friends is not talking to this one, but that one is talking to her. It gets so complicated. Boys just don't do that. We used to just fight and then become friends. Hell, my best friend at school became the boy I had...my toughest fight with, but it's different for my daughter, and I just think that her mother seems to be able to work through these things better than I could.'

> **Father:** 'The crying came from nowhere. I didn't know what to say to make the situation okay when she split from her boyfriend. Everything I said was wrong, and I just made it worse.'

Here lies the problem for fathers who are already traumatised by the whole drama and emotional thing that we would prefer to avoid, but we cannot walk away because they are our daughters. How can we possibly find the words, the answers, to our daughters' pain? You see, this is what we do in life – we solve problems, fix things, and try to make things better because that's what we do. Well, I have yet to meet a dad who was able to give good advice in such an emotionally charged situation. Ironically, and so importantly, is that, as fathers, we have unconsciously cut off our daughters from their male sides.

Just as we discussed boys being denied or dissuaded from developing their feminine sides, we can say the same of our daughters' male sides. The fact is that both sexes need a balance of both male and female traits, and these traits should not compete against each other. I concede that, culturally and historically, in many countries, male traits tend to dominate in society. So-called masculine traits – such as rational and calm thinking – against the feminine traits of emotional and caring are seen as more important in society. So, what we are denying our daughters is the ability to think temporarily like us, detach themselves emotionally from certain situations, and think about how to solve the dilemma or come across as confident and assertive even if they do not feel that way inside. Who better to teach this than their fathers, who have been doing just that for decades? Again, I stress that both our daughters and sons need to connect with their male and female inner selves in equal measure to feel whole. We can help our daughters to develop and use some of our more positive male traits when the time arises without losing the feminine traits that define them.

Fathers who talk to their teenage daughters' have informed that this doesn't have to be a hard thing to do, and you would be surprised just how much or how little your daughter will talk to you, depending on the topic. Some things will still remain off-limits because she would not dream of talking to you about it, anyway. Also, as men, once again, we are looking for ways to be in control, to fix things for our daughters when they struggle. Maybe our daughters just want us to listen, and they will find the solutions to their own problems, either by themselves or with the advice of their friends, family, and sometimes you. That's what growing up is about.

This is similar to some men's reactions to their partners wanting to have heart to hearts with them about where their relationships are going. We become tense, although we know the conversation needs to happen, but we find blocking techniques to avoid having to participate in these deep conversations. Our daughters frighten us much more than our wives due to our inherent needs to make things better – again, to fix things. My sisters had a very different type of relationship with my dad than I do with my daughter today. Perhaps the reason why we struggle as fathers is that we do not have templates. It is a testament to modern-day fathering that some daughters are able to approach their fathers to hold conversations, compared to our fathers, who seemed to have less of an outwardly emotional availability to our sisters.

So, this really is uncharted water for some of us as we try to reconnect with our teenage girls in the way we used to when they were little girls. It is the child who used to be known as 'daddy's girl' who needs Dad to provide emotional comfort, and we should embrace that, but the answer seems not too dissimilar from how we should deal with our partners and wives who need to talk, and that is to be there to listen and not try to fix the problems because we do not always have the solutions. We must learn to just listen to our daughters at times and try to avoid feeling that we are 'Mr Fix-its' all the time. Just be there for your daughter, and she will guide you as to what she needs.

The topic of boys really rattles a lot of fathers with whom I spoke, and reveals so much about our male upbringings and the need for such discussions among men of all persuasions. It is not lost on the fathers that Britain has the highest statistics in Europe for teenage pregnancies. The fathers fear that without adequate guidance, their daughters' life chances will be severely curtailed if they were to get pregnant at an early age. As fathers, they would feel a sense of failure, having not protected their daughters from becoming pregnant and not fulfilling their academic or life potentials. Fathers want their daughters to view their relationships with their partners or wives as the model for their daughters to which to aspire. In general, the increase in sexualised behaviour in society can minimise the importance of relationship building and maximise the acts of sexual gratification.

> **Father:** 'Tell me which one smiled and made a pass at you so I can go and thump him!'

This drew general approval around the country from fathers. When it comes to talking about boys, and in particular, those who do not show ambition and are steeped in street fashion, steam came out of some fathers' ears. Even with the conservative-speaking fathers who tended to use rational thinking in their discussions, you could see a visible change of attitude whilst talking about these types of boys. So many fathers subjectively felt the street mentality meant these boys struggled to secure or maintain mainstream jobs, and therefore, would not be good partner-material for their daughters or additions to their families. The saying, 'No one is good enough for my daughter,' is alive and kicking in the majority of men with whom I spoke, who were clear when it came to what they wanted for their daughters. The question is: do their daughters want the same boys their fathers aspire them to have?

The problem for some fathers who have chosen to leave so-called 'women's stuff' to their wives or partners over the years seems to be the main victims in this area. The daughters have not received lectures from these fathers about the dangers of testosterone-fuelled boys. After all, if these sudden warnings from fathers are not consistent in their relationship with their daughters over the years, they are likely to feel uncomfortable and become defensive at their unsolicited approaches. Funny how fathers' protection of their daughters changes to become much more targeted, specific, and manic as puberty sets in compared to when they were young children.

Could it be that we know what teenage boys are like because we were once teenage boys ourselves? Overall, our teenage daughters are intelligent and at a stage in their lives where they are at impressionable ages. They are inquisitive and questioning about the world in which they live, rather than just accept things as they are. Their eyes are open as they learn about the world and some of the injustices, in particular, the double standards that have been applied to women throughout history and in the home. They start to understand the power imbalance between men and women in all parts of society and how they relate to the opposite sex.

They formulate the foundations of their personalities and moral bases via their families, peer groups, and teachings at school or college, so you can image when fathers who have been absent from such debates start to lay down our authorities and expert opinions about boys without having proper conversations with our daughters, and they seem to be solely based on their views towards female and male behaviour. Such reactions from fathers can be seen in some of the comments I witnessed at a newly formed fatherhood group:

> **Father:** 'I warned her to stay away from Daniel. I don't like the look of him!...his backside is hanging from his trousers. He is not coming into my house...I couldn't even understand what the boy was saying to me so how is he going to get a job?'

Our attitude towards dress sense seems to have originated from our parents, whereby a pair of ironed trousers, polished shoes, and a nice shirt is a sign of respectability and ambition. We struggle with the modern 'street look' because our generation started with matching track tops and bottoms and trainers, but there did seem to be a common consensus amongst the 30-year-old fathers and the one quoted above that showing bare flesh or underpants with overhanging jeans is unacceptable. Interestingly, some of the younger fathers felt that the hanging jeans were getting too low, making the fashion borderline acceptable to them.

As time goes by, youth culture always seems to find another avenue with which to shock parents, and the more we are shocked, the more young people enjoy publicly parading what we do not like. This is youth culture and fashion. Of course, there is a huge generalisation being made by fathers towards teenage boys. The clothes worn do not necessarily represent the people or their ambitions in life – their clothes sometimes just represent the fashion of the day. Dress sense can be deceiving. The news has continually shown us that even when adults wear suits, it does not mean they are respectable or that they won't end up in jail. Surely, it is the person in the clothes that counts. With these attitudes of fathers who cannot or will not look past the clothes to see whether the boy has potential or is trouble, we know there is going to be tension at best and fireworks between father and daughter in their choice of a boy at the worst. This is especially true if your daughter actually likes a boy, you have decided is not for her, and you cuss his name every minute of the day.

We can and should take interest where our daughters are concerned, like school life, friends, gender equality or inequality, musical tastes, and food, long before boys come along. We then build our relationships with them at an early age, so that talking about boys becomes a natural part of our everyday discussions, rather than ignore their interests in life and take issue about boys all of a sudden.

As some fathers have stated, it would be better to start discussions at an early age as this helps you learn how to talk to your daughter. It is never too late to start talking to your daughter, but try to be non-judgemental and listen to her thoughts, otherwise, she will give up on you, and you will be closed out. As one father who has three daughters stated, 'It's probably advisable to start on less contentious issues than boys. Otherwise, you may end up arguing and end your attempt to talk even before it has begun.'

Other fathers agreed: 'Taking an interest in her life and helping her to make the right decisions in life when she is in doubt, reminding her how talented and brainy she is, goes a long way.' 'Talking about boy's working out the good from the bad and what a boy's intentions might be towards her can happen more naturally. That is, of course, if our daughters decide that they want to talk to us in the first place.'

As our daughters grow older, both parents – whether together or individually – need to reassure them about a number of areas in their lives. They will, of course, have confidence in certain areas, as girls of today are a different breed compared to 20 years ago, and with social media and Facebook, the world is a changing place, and they seem to understand the knowledge of information they can download at the touch of a button. Thinking independently and concentrating on their careers rather than being preoccupied with finding the right man, getting married, having children, and living happily ever after – these generations seem to put it on the back burner for later in life.

Girls and women of today understand that they have choices in life, and they do not have to depend on men to earn a living or survive financially in Britain. However, early teenage life is filled with so much uncertainty as they search for and negotiate their places in the home and at school and/or college. This is why we need to be around because the Internet will not teach them about life or healthy relationships, but we can help steer them through the murky waters of adolescence. On the flip side, there are traditional women who have brought up families and modern, career-minded women are no longer looking to settle down, choosing to practise the art of being independent instead, some by choice and others by circumstance. Those who are not through choice – such as by separation, divorce, or the man finding another partner – I believe are partly a by-product of failing men, and some women understanding that they cannot wait for a knight in shining armour to come along, as life must go on with or without a man.

A tribute to mothers

I could not end without a thought from one of the fatherhood groups and fathers splinted around the country, as a common thread seems to exist. Whether they are with their wives or have separated from them, they wanted me to pass this message on to all mothers. I hope I have been successful at capturing their words.

We want to acknowledge and thank you for all the positive, tireless, and vital roles made by our partners and wives in developing our daughters' personalities and characters. Through their unique experiences as women and the barriers they face in life, it is they who help our daughters through the minefields of life's challenges. As women growing up in a minority group in Britain, they are able to pass on critical advice, instil an inner determination and belief for our daughters to thrive and succeed in the worlds of work and home. They are truly role models for our daughters' successes in life.

A closing thought

Having listened to the experiences of fathers, it is clear that we can and do add to our daughters' lives in so many ways if we so choose. Fathers are saying is that a partnership between both parents and daughters will build a foundation for all our children, and we need to play our parts, too. Young women of today are much more self-assured than, say, my sister or mother's generation were at their age because we live in a time where women have higher aspirations. I want my daughter to stand on her own two feet, with or without a husband (as this will be the reality for some women) and know her extended family supports her all the way, to be as confident as possible, rather than placing limitations on her undoubted talents. She should feel like she can achieve, no matter the odds, able to give her best on her exams, in interviews, in projects at work, or in her own business, and have the confidence to choose a partner she believes will treat her with respect because she likes what she sees in the mirror every morning. We, as fathers, can acknowledge our affirmations towards our daughters need to be long-term as we support them in the areas of their lives and the loves they choose to pursue.

There are many contributing factors that build or damage our daughters' self-esteem. Some of these are our families' reputations in our communities, whether parents provide good role modelling, whether they understand the importance of encouragement and of praise when there is doubt in our daughters' minds, the types of friends, whether mature and studious or looking for trouble, promoting regular school attendance as this leads to good routines and qualifications, and communicating the possibilities in their lives.

We are aware that, so often, major contributing factors to our daughters' development are the types of parents they have from an early age, whether our attitudes towards gender are traditional and pronounced or more modern with room to manoeuvre and allow our daughters to define their development or hold them back, whether we are willing to allow our daughters to grow and explore life's opportunities, even if she wants to join the fire brigade. With our encouragement to push gender boundaries, our daughters will learn to look beyond their external looks and explore deeper into their souls to aspire and become the people they choose to be and not be held by the shackles of gender expectations.

From the Eyes of Children: What Are Dads Really Like?

'Bend the tree while it is young.'

– Common proverb

How do we cope as fathers?

It can be difficult to gauge how well we are doing as fathers. Our fathering roles are in transformation as we take on a more caring and leisurely role compared to our fathers before us. The gender divide in some, but not all, areas between our partners and ourselves is becoming less pronounced compared to our parents' generations. If you are lucky enough to have a partner, friend, or family member who can provide you with feedback on how you cope with modern-day fathering, that is great. However, all too often, our fathering is a matter of thinking on our feet, refereeing sibling rivalries, and disciplining our children. Multi-tasking (which we are useless at as we are all too often reminded by the opposite sex) leaves little space for us to reflect on how we deal with particular situations within our families.

It is a shame that the majority of fathers I spoke to do not feel they have enough time to reflect on their fathering to fine-tune their fathering skills, but in our busy lives, how can we gauge whether we are on track when it comes to our children's development and understand what they think about us? Well, there is another way: why don't we ask our children how they feel about our fathering?

I have spoken to children, aged six to 16 years old in small focus groups, and here is a summary of what they had to say about their fathers. Their answers are based on their observations and experiences, so they are subjective feelings and opinions of their fathers rather than scientific measurements. Their feedback provides us with interesting insight into the world of children and the impact we have on their lives as fathers.

Table – Results of focus groups

What do you like most about your dad?	What do you dislike most about your dad?	What makes a good father?
Takes me places.	Strict.	Takes me football/ swimming.
Makes me laugh.	Shouts at me.	Gives me pocket money.
Does fun stuff.	Too busy to play.	My role model.
Gives me treats.	Embarrasses me in public.	Being smart.
Gives me biscuits.	Short temper/no patience.	Sense of humour.
Gives me advice about friends and sport.	Slaps me on the bum.	Always there, and I feel safe.
Always there when I need him.	Lack of money.	Gives me hugs and kisses.

The above table gives you a quick glance at the topics discussed in the focus groups. See if some of the children's comments are familiar to you without taking it too personally.

What children like most about their dads

By far, the most popular answers were about fathers who made their children laugh and took them to fun places. Children enjoy going to the park, swimming, bowling, being accompanied on their weekend activities, eating out, and visiting friends. These activities and spending time with family all came out on the top of the list. However, long car trips were one of their least favourite pastimes. Time spent with their fathers meant they were not at home being told off for not completing their chores or homework or arguing with their brothers and sisters. Also, going to fun places meant that dad would be more relaxed, happy, and receptive to having fun.

The children liked and valued time together with their dads when they were more relaxed. The children understood the importance of getting Dad out of the house. They would push by trying to initiate an activity by taking ideas to Dad to get him to take them out. The children did not believe their dads realised how much they liked being taken out by them. Initially, some dads moaned about having 'other things' to do around the home, but the older children in the groups seemed more intuitive. They knew that once Dad was out and stopped worrying about 'other things', he became more relaxed and was able to enjoy the activity. As one teenager said: 'We can have fun with Dad, but we have to get him in the mood, first; you know, forget about paying the bills, work problems, and fixing things around our house – then he enjoys himself'. (15-year-old boy)

Such comments have far-reaching meanings, as the children identified that Dad needed to de-stress at times and acknowledge how important their time with their children was. Making suggestions as to where to go was their way of assisting Dad to relax and forget his problems. Play for these teenagers was not only about what they needed, but also what they identified as their dads' needs, too. However, work seems to be an important contributory factor as to whether parents can or cannot find the time to spend with their children. In particular, for fathers who work long hours in semi- and non-skilled professions.

> **Max:** 'I work long night shifts at work, so when I am sleeping, my kids are awake, and when they are sleeping, I am working. I would prefer to spend more time with them, but until I am able to get a better job, I have to make ends meet, so I also do some overtime. My sons sometimes complain, but what can I do? I tell him that Daddy will eventually find another job, and I will be able to play more football with them.'

What children dislike most about their dad

By far, the most talked-about topic was the dads' strictness. Asked what they meant by *strictness*, the children struggled at first to identify concrete definitions as it was based on their feelings around so many issues that had happened in their lives. What they were able to explain by using examples is that the dads' strictness was linked to them shouting, either at them or their siblings. The majority of children hated when their dads shouted at them, and they felt they would prefer for their dads to talk or even raise their voices but not shout at them. Mums were seen as having more patience and talking before they lost their tempers.

> 'Sometimes, my dad gets so mad with us, he shouts. He doesn't have much patience like mum does.' (12-year-old boy.)

All focus groups felt that dads tended to shout when they were frustrated or wanted their own ways. Shouting was seen as a way for dads to get instant responses from their children. However, there is a negative side to shouting at children. The children agreed that the dads did not shout every day, but when they did, it sometimes frightened them because they were not always expecting it.

> 'If my dad shouts, he is really serious, and we do as he says because we are frightened. (9-year-old girl).

Some children from the focus groups felt their dads had short tempers and argued a lot with their mums, family members, and/or friends. They felt their dads believed they were always right and everyone else was wrong. They had witnessed their dads wear down family members with their sides of the argument until they surrendered. These two boys were clear that they avoided conflict with their dads at all cost.

The focus groups were able to come up with some solutions found in the discussions held. For instance, some children mentioned they would like their dads to talk more often and explain rather than just shout at them over things they have done.

I feel the children are clearly saying that shouting at them is and should not be the only way for dads to communicate with their children. Otherwise, what the children learn from their dads is that, in order to be heard and get your own way, you should resort to shouting at people. Children also felt their dads could, at times, embarrass them in public, and different individuals within the focus groups told us stories. However, I did not sense their opposition to being embarrassed was as strong and serious compared to the discussion on the dads' strictness and shouting at them.

Other areas of complaints for both mums and dads are showing pictures of when they were younger to visitors and secretly not liking clothes bought for them by their dads and having to wear the clothes to please them. Teenagers, in particular, did not like being told off in public, as they felt adults' disapproving eyes focused on them. All of these stories were told in a more relaxed atmosphere, sharing stories, and at times, laughing at the shared predicaments into which their dads had placed them. The children felt that the biggest embarrassment of all was around fashion and music because the dads were out of touch and old fashioned. Dads often lectured their children about when music was 'real music' and words to a song were the most important thing and not the video. Oh, boy, did I feel old as I listened to the children and teenagers because I remembered saying the same things to my children!

The most embarrassing music choices made by dads is country and western and reggae revival music. Some of the teenagers said these types of music just put them to sleep as their parents sang and danced, using, as one girl described it, as 'old, slow-looking steps' along to their 'dinosaur tunes.' Ouch! That hurts. To make matters worse, during christenings, weddings, or family get-togethers, their parents often grabbed their arms whilst passing to dance with them to these types of music, which they did not even like. The children actually laughed and enjoyed talking about this topic, as one boy said, Teenagers find it difficult to understand why their dads are still wearing outdated hairstyles or clothes. Some children disagreed as their dads were into label or designer clothes, but these children were far and few between. The majority of children and teenagers took great joy in laughing at their fathers' dress senses, but when faced with the dilemma that money did not grow on trees, and if it was a choice between their dads continuing to wear their low budget, unfashionable clothes and their continuing to receive their preferences when it came to clothes or going to their weekend activities, they all agreed their dads should continue to sacrifice to ensure their own wardrobes were updated and activities continued.

The children also talked about the generation gap, just like we did in relation to our parents. They were adamant that although they loved their dads, they did not want to be as old as they were or have similar tastes in music or clothes. They truly believed that being 40 years old was ancient, and 50 years olds? Well, let's not even go there!

Are we our fathers?

I remember thinking the same things about my dad's dress sense and how it was so alien from my taste in clothes. Looking back, is it inevitable that we end up having our dads' ways, mannerisms, and outlooks in life? The very people we promised ourselves we would never become end up being the people who guide our parenting.

Maybe we just learn through having our own children that some of our parents' teachings were wiser than we thought at the time. I have a light-hearted joke, with my brother James that if we ever thought about growing tomatoes in our gardens like our dad used to, we could slap each other to bring us to our senses. As the years went by, my brother started talking about growing tomatoes, and I enjoyed slapping his face. However, my brother's reason for cultivating tomato plants makes sense, and it probably did to my dad at the time. Tomatoes are no longer cheap, and it would be cost-effective for his family if he were to grow his own. Maybe I should stop slapping his face and just accept that I am my dad's child, buy the tomatoes, plant them in my garden, and grow old gracefully.

On a serious note, so many fathers seem to take traits from their fathers without even realising it. Fathers known for having a lack of patience and short fuses were able to take a step back to explore the comments from their children. Ironically, our behaviour seems to mirror both our fathers and grandfathers in this respect.

Remember that we did not often see our fathers due to the long hours they worked, and when we did see them, they were either sleeping due to being tired or disciplining us for something we had done whilst they were at work. The old saying, 'Wait till your father gets home' was very real and scary.

Listening to the children complain about their fathers shouting at them or the strictness they experienced at times reminded so many fathers of their own childhood and the parenting they received. These fathers were not used to receiving feedback from children, but they appreciated and understood the importance of being aware of their children's frustration and not taking it out on them. I think a clue for us fathers moving forward laid in the boy that said Mum took her time to explain what he was doing was wrong.

Forgotten childhood?

Have we really forgotten what it's like to be children? It can be a fun-filled experience but also a powerless and misunderstood period of our lives. I certainly remember being the seventh out of eight children and having little say. Come to think of it, I had no say in what we watched on TV, what I ate for dinner, and what games we played, but I still had great fun. Childhood has changed from the days when children were allowed to play on the streets with their friends all day long, only coming home for food or drink. Those days were truly a time of perceived freedom for children when they felt they could go anywhere and still make it home in one piece. Today, more home-based activities around technology and child-focused, structured activities outside the home have taken over.

We are a generation of parents who spend much more time with our children than past generations, yet international studies highlight that far from enjoying their life, our generation of children are far less content. Such is the state of affairs that UNICEF has commented that although some children live in the richest countries around the world, their emotional wellbeing is suffering. The UNICEF report (February 2007) on the wellbeing of children and young people in 21 industrialised countries concluded that children in the United Kingdom ranked at the bottom of the wellbeing assessment.

For the first time, there was a report that measured and compared overall child wellbeing by using 40 separate indicators from relative poverty, child safety, educational achievement and opportunity to play, all of which are brought together to paint a picture of the lives of children around the world. Here are some of the findings:

- Northern-eastern countries dominate the top half of the table, with child wellbeing at its highest in the Netherlands, Sweden, Denmark, and Finland. The UK and the United States find themselves at the bottom of the rankings.

- The report found some interesting similarities with the results of my children's focus groups. For instance, one of the dimensions looked at by the UNICEF report was regarding children's social relationships. Relationships with family and friends matter a great deal to children in the here and now and are important to long-term psychological development.

- The percentage of parents who spent time 'just talking to their children' several times a week ranged from approximately 90% in Hungary and Italy to less than 50% in Canada and Germany.

- The percentage of children who reported that their peers were kind and helpful towards them varied from a high 80% or more in Switzerland and Portugal to less than 50% in the Czech Republic and the UK.

- Fewer than 15% of young people reported being drunk on two or more occasions. In the Netherlands, the figure rose to over a quarter and in the UK, to almost a third.

- The percentage of young people (aged 15) who reported having used cannabis varied widely from less than five per cent in Greece and Sweden to more than 35% in the UK, Switzerland, and Canada.

- All countries had weaknesses that needed to be addressed. The report did not attempt to explain each country's individual ranking, but it is intended to stimulate national debate and encourage countries to address areas in which they had room for improvement.

- Children's subjective senses of wellbeing appeared to be markedly higher in the Netherlands, Spain, and Greece and markedly lower in Poland and the UK.

It is not often that, as parents, we have an opportunity to read a non-governmental, independent document that focused on the issues that affected our children. We need to take heed of the findings of this independent body and address our children's wellbeing.

I noticed that politicians from countries that reflected badly were quick to denounce the findings as inaccurate or state that, since the study had been completed, they had made major strides in some of the areas mentioned and praised their own work to counter child poverty. Other counties also fared badly, but they were not as industrialised or as rich a nation as the UK. They also had less disposable income with which to entertain their children. The sad fact is that I could not find a dimension in the report in which the UK did really well, and that was both shocking and an indictment of our attitudes towards children and how we treat them.

A Closing thought

As a father, listening to the children was an interesting experience. Of course, at times, their demands were unrealistic, but also, at times, they were clear about how fathering had an impact on them. As they spoke, I felt I was running through the scenarios I have had with my own children questioning my actions. Am I too impatient? Do I play with my children enough? Are my clothes really that bad? Do I really raise my voice that much (surely, they are exaggerating)? So, in every one of us, there are probably areas at which we can look and on which we can improve. Our children are not authorities on fathering, but they do have unique insights as they are on the receiving ends of our decisions and moods.

I think the most significant issues to come out of this focus group was the time we spent with our children. Whether second- or third-generation fathers, the message from our children is clear: please find time to spend with us because we like spending time with you, and once you are with us, you tend to forget about life's difficulties and enjoy the time we spend together.

There is, however, an important issue that I feel plays a big part in whether we are able to spend more time with our children. I mentioned this in the chapter **To Read or Not to Read with Your Children, That is the Question**, how long working hours and work conditions can affect the amount of reading and homework fathers are able to do with their children.

This also applies to how much leisure time fathers are able to commit to their children if working unsociable hours.

Many of the fathers to whom I spoke on this subject had a working-class background, mainly semi-skilled workers who work long, unsocial hours with a shift pattern. The professional fathers tended to work a fixed set of hours but had a work flexibility that allowed them to take time off to suit their family commitments.

> **Robert:** 'I don't work weekends, just nine to five, Monday to Fridays. That allows me to take my kids to gymnastics and football on a Saturday. I can also take leave during their summer holidays, but I really like the fact that I can put the children to bed at night. I have a friend who cannot do that because of the long hours he works.'

We do need to take our children's opinions and the UNICEF study seriously because we are talking about our present and future relationships with our children. We all want to have long, successful relationships with our children well into adulthood. If you are truly blessed with children who have good hearts because you have worked on your relationship building with them and have given them your time and love, your children might reciprocate this and look after you in old age, rather than send you to live in a retirement home.

Thank you, mums

A big thanks to the mums who allowed their children to participate and dish the dirt on their partners/husbands. You understood that their comments were important for us as fathers to hear and grow.

Back to the Future – Grandfathers Speak

'What a bargain grandchildren are. I give them my loose change, and they give me a million dollars' worth of pleasure.
– Gene Perret

The missing link

Having met so many fathers whilst writing this book, I felt like there was something missing, but I couldn't put my finger on it until one day, I was speaking to Justin. He has always been a fountain of advice about life experiences for me and a pillar in the community, so when he speaks, you listen. He said something during our conversation that struck me to the core, and all of a sudden, I had the answer to what I was looking for. He was standing before me, and as I listened intently, he said the following: 'It is my duty as a granddad to protect and help my grandchildren to grow healthy and to be successful.'

It was at that moment I realised what was missing from my book: Justin and the other grandfathers. Their views on the topic of fatherhood had not been included. After all, they were the first generation of parents responsible for bringing up and moulding the second and third generation fathers of today. I thought it might be interesting to find out their experiences while parenting and how they see and view parenting today. There is an estimated 14,000,000 grandparents in Britain, and research informs us that a third of our population will be grandparents by 2022

These first-generation immigrants from the Caribbean and Africa tend to shun the limelight and are even more invisible than the British born second and third generation fathers. They possess wisdom beyond our wildest dreams, and most importantly, their stories allow us to see how attitudes and methods towards parenting have changed throughout the decades.

According to recent research, adolescents aged between 11 and 16 found that children do better in life if their grandparents play a big part in their upbringing. The survey said that children who had a close relationship with their grandparents could be protected against the worst effects of traumas, such as divorce or a family breakdown.

Armed with my discussion questions and a second-generation father to accompany me, we met with the first of many grandfathers at the Green Light Youth Centre in Bow East London. The meeting proved to be very humbling, and at the same time, it was one of the highlights of our search for guidance as to how present and future fathers can improve their parenting and share their learning. It is time for us to listen to the stories on life and parenting from the missing link to this book: the grandfathers.

Growing up in the Caribbean

The grandfathers recounted their experiences growing up as young boys in the Caribbean and Africa. Either their parents brought them up, or another very common practice was for grandparents or an aunt to take on the responsibility. This custom was not unusual; it was a way of utilising grandparents and ensuring the extended family played a significant child-rearing role.

Another fascinating aspect was that children were expected to be courteous towards adults at all times. Many grandfathers spoke of having to say good morning or how do you do when passing adults in the streets or in town. Not greeting an adult in the correct manner could lead to a slap over the head or a complaint to your parents, which was to be avoided at all costs. Some children would even plead with the adult they'd offended not to tell their parents because they would face another slap over the head when they returned home.

The grandfathers also recollected not being able to interrupt adults' conversations whilst talking, as this again, this would be seen as the height of rudeness, and possible chastisement could follow. Children's behaviours were seen as reflections of their parents' standing in the community. Children who lacked manners or were known to misbehave were gossiped about and sometimes shunned by other children. As one grandfather said, 'Manners went a long way, and rudeness brought you nothing but trouble.' Stepping out of line was at your peril as beatings from your father were commonplace. The objects used to administer punishment varied, but the belt, slipper, and tree branch were substituted if a belt was not at hand.

> **Grandfather:** 'My father was a man of few words, and he did not hesitate to use his large belt made from leather when disciplining us. Strong punishment and discipline were institutionally and culturally based throughout Caribbean families, communities, and schooling. Pupils at school and on the streets addressed all adults by their surname and never by their first name, as this was seen as being disrespectful.'

One of the grandfathers spoke about being the eldest out of 11 children and having to look after his siblings when his parents went into the fields to harvest. He was expected to keep an orderly house and could get into trouble if he did not take his responsibility seriously. One grandfather spoke about how he was brought up by his grandparents. His grandmother was head of the household when it came to everyday issues, but his grandfather made the big decisions around finance and disciplining the children. So, this was the foundation these grandfathers had learned from their parents on parenting: strong family and Christian values wrapped around strong disciplinary boundaries if children stepped out of line.

I can honestly say I did not meet one grandfather who said that communication with their fathers was a natural and free-flowing event. In fact, the attitude of 'children should be seen and not heard' was the prevailing model at the time. Whereas children of today are, on the whole, free to express their feelings and ideas to their parents, this was not the case 70 years ago. This would explain their strict and disciplinarian approach towards us.

A few grandfathers spoke with fondness about going to church on a Sunday morning, dressed in what was known as their Sunday best. Sundays were – and still are – viewed by their generation as a day of rest and family, when you pray and thank God for what you have and for protecting you from harm. This is followed by dinner with the family and long conversations about all kinds of topics, but mainly gossip about people in the town.

Coming to Britain and facing the obstacles

For these grandfathers, the journey and early years in Britain are well-documented in books and documentaries, but what is relevant to us as fathers today is that these grandfathers never planned to stay in Britain for more than five years, much less bring up families here.

One grandfather said that he wanted to return home within six months of being in Britain after seeing the smoke-filled chimneys, the fog, and feeling the cold brick walls in his room during the winter months. Unfortunately, the majority could not afford the fare home due to the low wages (a few were earning £5 per week in 1959) they received. We are talking about the 1950s and early 1960s when real hardship existed for these men and women who had left their homelands for a better standard of life. Survival was the name of the game, and having enough money to find shelter (often living in one rented room where you slept, cooked, ate, and washed) and put food in their bellies was considered a triumph in the right direction.

Fathers today cannot imagine living in such an alien environment, having to learn the customs and systems of a country so different from their own, and to make matters worse, it was a totally hostile climate and people compared to the ones they were used to back home, but these grandparents wanted an opportunity, not only to better themselves but to help the Mother Country rebuild after the terrible pounding it had taken from Hitler's bombs and the destructive V2 rockets. The determination to succeed was strong within them, and through their tough upbringing and Christian values, they decided to persevere and overcome the immense barriers placed before them.

For instance, the grandfathers spoke about the weather in Britain being so cold in the 1950s they would get lost in the fog, trying to reach home. One grandfather told us a story about his tea breaks at work being shortened because, by the time he was ready to drink his flask of tea, it was icy. Another grandfather spoke about his hands being so numb he would lose his gloves, not realising they had dropped out of his hands. I remember one of my uncles telling me that his hands were so frozen, he could not turn the key in his front door to enter.

Financial survival and the world of work

Men and women who possessed qualifications or a trade were not permitted to work in these areas. Most companies were not willing to acknowledge their qualifications, and this meant that the jobs on offer paid much less than they had anticipated. The wages were low, but they were able to save to send for their wives or girlfriends to join them in Britain. What was left went towards paying the rent and buying food. Once children had come along, the grandfathers felt their plans to get rich quick and return home had become distant dreams. They felt a duty to stay in Britain to provide for their families. We are talking about the mid-1960s and early 1970s, and employment conditions had improved due to trade unions and government legislation, but most of the grandfathers were still trying hard to make ends meet as promotions to more senior positions were still being blocked, irrelevant of their having gained British qualifications or on the job training. Some grandfathers see parallels to Britain then when compared to now, as they were doing semi- or non-skilled work and earning low wages, similar to other recently settled immigrant populations.

Ironically, although their wages were low, the jobs were plentiful. A few grandfathers remembered vividly that you could walk into a factory and secure another job during your lunchtime and start the next day compared to now. A few grandfathers received benefits from the then Employment Exchange for a few weeks until they had found new jobs, but this was for no longer than a month at a time.

Some of the grandfathers proudly announced they have never claimed unemployment benefits in the whole of their lives. These grandfathers found it difficult to understand some long-term unemployed people in Britain today, as they felt that taking a job for your pride was better than not having one at all. They unanimously agreed that unless a person was too old or seriously ill, he should be working, otherwise they would view him as lazy. They had a common consensus around the importance of work for the soul and the biblical dangers of idle hands (doing nothing all day), especially amongst the young. Therefore, they felt it was the duty of every man to work for a living and not beg, borrow, or steal his way through life – which felt like a biblical lecture – but such views did show the influence of their upbringing around having high work ethics. The grandfathers felt that, through the decades, the government had allowed people to become dependent on state benefits, leading to masses of unemployed unable to re-adjust to working life. Long-term benefits meant that their rent and council taxes were paid for, leading to people not having the incentive to work.

One grandfather spoke emotionally about visiting his hometown in the Caribbean some time ago and meeting some of his friends with whom he had grown up and gone to school. He explained that his friends had not moved on economically, lived in the same place, and had few career opportunities ahead of them. He then realised how fortunate he was in deciding to come to Britain. At times, he faced racism, such as landlord notices on doors stating, 'No Blacks, no Irish, and no dogs,' but obstacles were part of life, and they did not stop him from advancing in life. His message to the habitually unemployed – not to those who cannot work – is that they should be thankful and feel lucky they have job prospects, whether they like what is on offer or not, because his old friends from the Caribbean would welcome the chance to take any type of job on offer as they had grown up with strong work ethics and not working feels like failing.

Back in the 1960s, there was a strong sense that, as men, they were the breadwinners and the main providers for their family, although some wives tended to return to work once some type of informal childcare had been secured. A popular arrangement was for their upstairs neighbours to keep an eye on their children whilst Mum was at her part-time work. So, although the so-called breadwinner model existed, the women helped financially. I expected to hear that traditionally, the women stayed at home whilst the men worked, but as one grandfather said, 'Our women are tough. They worked hard in the Caribbean and worked even harder in Britain once the children were a little older and able to take care of each other.'

Childcare

The grandfathers' experiences varied, as some went to work and their partners or wives stayed home to look after the children, but some who were nurses or in other professions worked just as many hours as their husbands. Women in the 1960s and 1970s tended to provide exclusive, informal childcare in the family or community with little assistance from the men. However, if you had a large family, which tended to be the norm, to pay £2 per child towards childcare was seen as too expensive. So, it was cost-effective for women to stay at home and rear the children.

At one stage, all of the grandfathers had children who were looked after by family or close friends rather than a formal set-up, as these tended not to last. For example, a grandfather explained that he had allowed a non-family female to look after his children at her home but was unhappy with the care provided, so he pulled his children out. The grandfathers all agreed that their experiences throughout the years was that the best type of childcare was from family members, as they cared for their children as they would have cared for their own.

Interestingly, the grandfathers of today look after children much more now than they did whilst bringing up their own children, when the childcare was, in the main, the responsibility of their partners and/or wives. How times have changed – some grandfathers looked after their grandchildren regularly or as and when they were needed to lend a hand. As one grandfather explained, 'I have more time on my hands now as a pensioner compared to when I had to provide for my family by working long hours.' Another grandfather said, 'As a grandparent, I feel much more relaxed than when I had my own children, as the pressure to survive and make money to buy food was constant. So, I enjoy spoiling my grandchildren and then giving them back to my daughter.'

There does seem to be a more relaxed feeling among the grandfathers whilst looking after their grandchildren. They talk about being less disciplined with them in a way they could not be with their own children. When talking to grandfathers, there was a general consensus that with age, the passage of time, and changing attitudes regarding men participating in playing and child-rearing. They had softened and had a more easygoing approach with their grandchildren. I can personally vouch for that. I will never forget – I was approximately 20 years old, and my father was sleeping on the sofa. My five-year-old niece, Nadine, had decided to sit on his stomach and bounce gently up and down. I had kittens, and I feared the worst for her, as waking up Dad from his sleep – well, let's just say that you didn't dare do it and expect him to be happy. My warning came too late, and I remember standing there, frozen, helpless, and expecting my niece to be swiftly chastised. My dad woke up, smiled gently, and asked, 'What are you doing, Nadine?'

Nadine said, 'I'm playing horses, and you are the horse.' At that point, I stopped holding my breath and stared at the two of them in disbelief. What a cheek, I thought. If any of my brothers or sisters had tried such a stunt, we would have received a slap.

There seems to be something magical about grandchildren that melts our parents' hearts in a way we could not whilst growing up in a more tactile, relaxed, flexible, and fun approach that I do not remember receiving from my dad. Maybe the pressure of working long hours, trying to make ends meet, and producing well-mannered children made their outlooks when it came to their children different. At the same time, they were trying to educate us in the school of hard knocks and felt it necessary to prepare us for a hard time living in Britain. Grandchildren and discipline are the responsibility of the parents and not theirs. Having been released from this role means that they can concentrate on getting to know their grandchildren and make them happy.

Financial difficulties and pardner savings

Our financial education in Britain was totally different compared to that of our parents' generations. They learned to save for the things they needed rather than wanted. Our generation tends to purchase items whether we have the money or not. Impulse buying on credit rather than saving in order to purchase is commonplace. Our parents had to be creative; a part of the hostile culture and practices meant that many banks would not loan them money; hence the creation of the pardner was born. A pardner is a form of savings, mainly among a combination of close friends and family. Each week, you put in the same amount of money as your group members. In an agreed payment order and saving period, the lump sum goes to a group member until all members eventually receive an interest-free lump sum. This allows people to purchase fridges, furniture, prams, paraffin heaters, and the like. The bigger the group, the bigger the cash payments received, but the longer it would take to receive the lump sums.

However, it was important that people did not get too greedy and allow the group to have members who were inconsistent with their financial contributions or repayment, and this is where the trust towards each other had to be earned to keep the financial flow strong, which allowed others to borrow at later dates.

> **Grandfather:** 'There were times when a member would fall on hard times, and the treasurer would arrange for a payment swap with another member of the group to allow for that person to receive payment much quicker. The foundation and popularity of pardners were based on the banks refusing to loan...us money, so we depended on our community to think of creative ways to generate money to pay for life's necessities.'

The grandfathers view of modern-day credit cards, loans, and the attitude of 'buy now pay later' received savage criticism. They believed the art of saving for what you need seems to have been replaced by impulse buying or desire rather than need. They saw many families getting into trouble and being tempted by credit and loans they just could not afford to pay back. They believed that the expectation of what people wanted and what they could realistically afford was misguided. They were sympathetic to modern-day working families because the cost of living and associated services had rocketed since their time as parents. Money has become so important for our survival that people can become fixated on trying to earn more and more, but money does not necessarily bring happiness. One grandfather said that he was happier in the '70s when he had less money because of the closeness, community spirit, and the help they had given to each other compared to now.

The cost of living was lower, the community cohesion was stronger, and it ensured that everyone looked after each other during hard times. He believed that people had become so private and proud about life and their money situations that you heard about their struggles when the bailiffs were at their doors. He called for families to stop hiding behind their feelings of shame and seek out one another's help in times of need. He spoke openly about the exchange of food between families and friends during hard times. Of course, people had their pride, and they did not want to inconvenience people too much, but the community all knew each other and that they would eventually have the chance to help another family soon.

> **Grandfather:** 'When we were young, we did not have the credit and buying power like people have today, but if we did, it would be interesting to see what would have happened...Would we have given into the temptation of plastic and spent or would we have continued saving for the things we needed?'

Modern-day discipline

The grandfathers believed that children nowadays are 'too unruly', and parents have become too soft with their children, leading to the blurring of the lines between what are the adult and children's roles. They are appalled at the children's talking back to and swearing at their parents, and they strongly believe that parents need to tell their children to 'fix up'. They believe that parents have become too soft, preferring to be their children's friends rather than their parents, and this is a dangerous blurring of boundaries between child and parent. They all come from a generation in which children should be seen and not heard and should show unconditional courtesy and respect to adults. They may have a point, as a recent survey in Britain found that respect for elders is on the decline. Around four in five people believe that respect for older generations has declined over the last ten years.

> **Grandfather:** 'In those days, we were not sitting around, thinking about or reading new parenting methods or being child-centred like you guys are today. Our jobs as fathers was to work hard and get on with the disciplining of our children, especially the boys who would push the boundaries when we were not around. But it was all I knew at the time, as that's how my dad had disciplined me as a boy.'

They left their biggest criticisms not for the parents, but the government, who they felt have taken away the parents' power to decide how to discipline their own children. A number of grandparents I met, either in groups or individually, were partly familiar with the Children's Act 1989. Prior to the Children's Act, the chastisement of children, whether right or wrong, was, overall, seen as a private family matter. With the creation of the Children's Act, children's rights came to the forefront.

One grandfather explained that the Act was supposed to mark a new period whereby the attitude and behaviour of adults towards children would change from a Victorian attitude of children being seen and not heard to one of mutual communication and understanding. Interestingly, a large number of grandfathers admitted that, in hindsight, their chastisement of their children was, at times, too harsh. However, they also felt that the government's intrusion into child discipline marked the beginning of the tilting of the balance of power too much in favour of the child. Parents have become immobilised when disciplining, and in particular, smacking their

169

children. A few group members spoke about parents deciding to steer clear of smacking their children because they feared social service intervention and surveillance of their parenting skills. In turn, some children know they have more power than ever before, and they push the boundaries with their parents in the knowledge that they can seek recompense from the authorities if their parents cross the line.

This topic really got the various groups thinking about modern-day parenting and who was in charge of the children's welfare – the parents or the council? How did the state judge which parents were doing a competent job, did ethnicity or class play a part in that judgement, and who would do the judging? Do parents know their parenting boundaries around smacking their children, or has the state made the boundaries confusing to parents?

The majority of grandfathers believe that the government needs to take a more arm's length approach when assisting parents to reclaim lost ground where discipline and controlling their children was concerned whilst protecting children who are at risk. They acknowledged that there are parents who are cruel to their children and the local authorities are right to take action against them. They believed that parents regaining some form of authority over their children is one of the biggest challenges they see ahead for modern parenting because, without the boundaries being reset for children and teenagers, they feared a general lack of respect for authority and adults, which would continue to increase and eventually lead to young people feeling they were above any rules set down by adults, and mass chaos would end up being the order of the day.

Thankfully, they are not advocating a return to using the belt on children or other forms of physical punishment. They acknowledged that hitting children may have been the way in times gone by, but this is not the answer for the best method of modern-day parenting. One grandfather admitted to me in private that his use of the belt wasn't the way anymore, and he realised it was wrong. He wished he had stopped using the belt earlier on with his children, but he struggled to think of other methods to discipline his children. This was pleasing to hear as I have either witnessed or been told so many horror stories regarding this. However, some grandfathers did advocate for traditional methods of punishment to be reinstated to regain control over our youth, but they were clear that times have changed, and with it, methods of discipline and new, less severe methods should be used for effective parenting.

For instance, they agreed with smacking but not beating children. Some acknowledged that they have observed their grown-up children using various methods of punishment, such as banning the playing of computer games for a set period, being grounded, or missing parties, which sometimes gets the desired effect. As a parent, you have the power to decide when to start or finish the punishment period. They were clear that there are times to 'order' children and times to 'reason' with them.

Some grandparents felt that national service or boot camp for some of the more out of control teenagers who have no regard for the laws of the land should seriously be considered. If they do not listen to their parents, the police, or the courts, they should face a more regimented type of discipline structure. Others felt that strong discipline started and belonged at home and that it was not just the state's responsibility. One grandparent said he'd sent his son back to Jamaica because he needed stronger discipline and more structure in his life. His son went to live with his grandparents, and school was an extension of the families' strict discipline. He felt that his, at the time, 15-year-old son was getting involved with the wrong crowd and was too headstrong to listen to anyone. He could see trouble ahead, and he wanted to avoid his son ending up in prison.

The practice of sending children or grandchildren home occurs on other Caribbean islands and in African and Asian communities, although it is less common amongst British born parents descendant from these continents. The families from abroad are almost like international extended family rescue services when the parent feels their children need a new structure that is not just based on discipline but another way of life to broaden their minds as to how other children live and the hard routines they have. Being a part of the family and helping out with the chores – including cooking and looking after younger family members. To do these chores is part the extended family looking after them and their expectations of the children – without earning pocket money as a part of their efforts abroad – will save them from further harm.

The wise men

The grandfathers believed the answer to parenting was the extended family or network of family and friends. Uncles, aunts, close friends, and parents provide wraparound care for a child. What these grandfathers are talking about is not dissimilar from that of the Caribbean and African family setups in which they were brought up. They believe that parents – and in particular, young parents – would benefit from the practical support and wisdom grandparents could offer. I met grandfathers who made conscious efforts to communicate with their children. They believed the lack of communication with their parents whilst growing up was detrimental to their childhood development and their learning how to be parents. It is no coincidence that these grandfathers get on very well with their grown-up children and their partners and/or wives, and they have consciously spent time cultivating their relationships with their children throughout the years.

I found that the grandfathers who had difficult relationships with their grown-up children were the ones who struggled to communicate to find a middle ground, taking on some of the traditional traits of their fathers and their fathers before them. In those relationships, communication was limited to a few words, usually to order them around rather than ask how they had spent their days.

However, grandparents do have modern-day obstacles that may prove difficult in their quests to share their wisdom. The modern-day perception towards the elderly, especially in Western countries, tends to be negative. We live in a society whereby technology seems to have rendered the elderly obsolete, and the elderly are left feeling as if they have no real tangible function in life. With the increased advancement of information technology, the young believe computers hold all the answers to life's queries. In days gone by, elders were considered knowledgeable, and they were sought after by the young to share that knowledge. The elderly were treated with great respect and reverence, and their library-like wisdom was held in high esteem. Unfortunately, information and knowledge are now but a Google search away. One grandfather illustrated this by trying to advise his daughter on childcare, but she preferred to check on the computer, talk to her friends, and read present-day specialists on the subject of teething. He felt useless and soon realised he would have to wait patiently to see when he might be considered of use.

His feelings are common among new grandfathers but not necessarily the norm. They may start by trying to negotiate their roles in the family, but this will soon become clear once babysitting duty starts, following the parents' inevitable return to work. It is at this point they are likely to become more involved with their grandchildren, and their suggestions may be received more readily when their grown-up children finally realise they know what they are talking about. I truly believe that some grandparents hold some of the answers to so many of life's problems simply because they have life experience, have been down so many blind alleys, and learned about life the hard way. As a society, we do not harness their wisdom as much as we could to benefit our lives – what a waste of such an important and knowledgeable generation.

This is why, as I was writing this book, I realised that grandfathers were the missing link to understanding the different eras of parenting.

Of course, all of their methods are not effective or right, for that matter, but isn't there something special about combining their experience of boundaries and discipline with modern-day parenting, one that combines effective communication with the deep need for parental role modelling at a time when children and teenagers need guidance?

I so strongly believe in the combined strength of this generational partnership and how it can benefit both elderly and young fathers that I am in the process of starting such a group. I hope, by the time this book is published, the group has been established and is providing a generational advice and support system for each other. This generational project is how both old and young could come together in mutual respect to learn from each other about life, relationships, and parenting. I have met enough grandparents who feel underused when asked if they would like to give more to their communities.

A few words of advice

Irrelevant of race or culture, I have asked every father I have met, either in a planned manner or through chance: what is the secret to being an effective father? This question has driven me through the writing of this book because out there – and now, in this book – there are answers to this question. Colour, ethnicity, class, rich or poor – it does not seem to matter or dictate whether someone is an effective father or not but, the effort they are willing to commit and their openness to new ideas is.

Parenting through the years

We were not born with all the much-needed attributes to be fantastic parents. We learn through our upbringings and what we witness and process throughout our lives. We store the parts of parenting we like and discard the parts we do not like. No one individual is a perfect father, so we learn new ideas and approaches as we go along. The more open and receptive we are to learning from each other, the better we will be as fathers within our families and communities. The better fathers we become, the more educated and rounded children we bring into the world to, hopefully, continue our families' legacies.

Throughout the years of being fathers and then grandfathers, the men have a unique outlook on the world that has changed so much since they were young boys growing up in the Caribbean and Africa. Their ingredients for being effective fathers are not based on opinions plucked from the sky or TV programmes. These ideas are real-life, tried and trusted ideas. It does not mean they are perfect or that they have always done things the right in their lives. Through life's trials and errors, these ideas have allowed them to be more effective fathers and grandfathers.

Of course, not all fathers feel that they have done perfect jobs, but it is a testament to them that they see their adult children and grandchildren on a regular basis and have healthy relationships with them. They must have done something – no, many things – right for the relationships to still be going. When I think of my young children and look at these grandfathers, I also wonder if my children, along with my future grandchildren, will continue to visit me in my old age; I certainly wish for them to do so. The glint in the grandfathers' eyes as they speak about their grandchildren was there for all to see. It is a sense of accomplishment and pride only grandparents can explain. No matter what they have endured in their lives, their grown-up children value their input and practical assistance with their children.

Communicating rather than lecturing

This leads us to one of the major relationship changes between parents and their grown-up children over the last 30 years: embracing your children even when they have grown-up and moved on. In order to keep the foundations of your relationship, lectures need to decrease, and adult communication and discussion must increase.

> **Grandfather:** 'If you can treat your adult children in a positive manner, they will always look forward to visiting you, but if you just continue to lecture them like they are still teenagers, they will think that because they are not children anymore, they don't need the hassle every time they visit.'

After all, they are now adults, making their own decisions in life. If they feel that a visit is more of a lecture on how they should be running their lives, they will keep visits down to a minimum. There is an art to communicating and providing advice through a two-way conversation rather than a one-way lecture.

Setting an example

Grandfathers were clear that one of the main components of fatherhood is setting a good example for your children. Demonstrating good behaviour, discipline, love, and a healthy work ethic will ultimately lead to your children following in your footsteps. Also, if your family and friends are similar to you and have ambition, achieving will seem natural to your children as they grow because everyone around them is doing the same.

Importance of community

The grandfather group felt the community spirit that had galvanised them in the late 1950s and throughout the '60s and '70s is sadly missing. The community spirit that existed had been based on mutual respect and an acknowledgement that they were all relatively new to Britain and needed to stick together. Dangers lay outside of the community from groups such as the Teddy Boys, and to a larger extent, from the skinheads and National

Front, so sticking together – whether Jamaican, St Lucian, or Kenyan – was the order of the day. People looked out for each other in many ways, and this was not based on just blood ties but also on close friendships within the community.

It was common to call adults uncle or aunt, and you were not even sure if they were your biological relations or not but you knew their relationship with your family was strong and enduring. Your across the hall neighbour with whom you not only shared a house but childcare, food, and hospitality was a mini interdependent culture magnified on a much larger scale when you opened the door and went outside.

Grandfather: 'I look around today and see that apart from people's families and close friends, people are not mixing, not supporting each other. They close their doors and keep to themselves. That was never our way. That is very English to do, that keeping yourself private, exchanging niceties, and that's it. If we want to be strong, we need to stick together and help each other through the tough times. So many people helped me through life, especially when I was between jobs or ill, and I helped others when I was strong and working. You don't forget what people do for you. I think our children, who were born here, are very English in some ways and don't even realise it. That's why I think people have become very private. They have taken on the majority culture, but I think they need to stop moving far away from their extended families because who will help you when you are sick, or you have an emergency? Listen, I am an old man, but when things start to go wrong in life, it is your family that rallies round to keep you afloat. Yes, you have your arguments, but you have to move on and try not to hold grudges, so don't forget them – they are the only family you have.'

Don't bring the police to my door

The reputation of the family was all-important, and our parents made it clear to us that we should not bring the police to their doorstep. The family shame and what others would say about them meant that we were expected to behave in public and maintain the family's reputation at all times, no matter what. Reputations take a long time to build and a short time to fall, and this was drummed into our heads at an early age so no one could say they did not know. The disappointment of damaging your family's reputation could lead to severe consequences. Several grandfathers explained, in an animated manner, their attitude on this subject matter.

> **Grandfather:** 'If the children shame me up, I would tell them don't bother coming home if you know what's good for you.'

> **Grandfather:** 'I made it clear that if the police come to my house, the children need not come home; otherwise, I would be the one the police would be arresting for murder. Go and live somewhere else as it is clear you cannot live by my rules.'

The grandfathers reflected on their ongoing message – some would say threat – to their children about what they expected from them in public and the consequence if they got into trouble with the law or other types of authorities. If push came to shove, they did not believe they would actually throw their children out, but the direct threat of what they might do seemed to be enough to keep their children out of trouble.

Don't raise your hand to your women

Two women are killed every day in Britain through domestic violence at the hands of their partners or ex-partners. In over 50% of known domestic violence cases, children are also directly involved. The issue of domestic violence came up within the groups with which I met, and this is seen as one of the most disrespectful and unacceptable behaviours a man can perpetrate on his partner. Although government legislation is making violence towards women in the home unlawful and such violence within the home is becoming socially unacceptable, we know that violence towards women still continues.

As one grandfather put it, 'If your children see you raising your hand to your wife, they might think it is okay to do this and will copy you when they grow... up.' This is a good point, as you will find that perpetrators or victims of domestic violence have either witnessed violence or were victims of violence whilst growing up.

Their love for Britain

There was a unanimous agreement amongst the grandfathers when it came to the opportunities Britain had given to them over the years. They have seen – and still see – Britain as a country with opportunities if you are willing to work hard. They even joked that if you are struggling, this country will help you to get back on your feet, but some people take this literally and do not continue to work. They feel that the help from the state is more than you would get from a lot of countries, but it angered them that people would take advantage of and abuse the system.

> **Grandfather:** 'The system is flawed because the country helps people when they are down, but there are so many lazy people who don't want to help themselves because the state will do it for them.

Their views on having a strong work ethic have been programmed into them from an early age by their families. Working hard was something they were expected to do, and a sense of duty was not an issue. They firmly believe that a part of life is to overcome obstacles. Although some people tried to make their lives difficult early on in Britain, they were in the minority. They refused to accept this and persevered in order to reach their goals in life. The grandfathers felt that younger men needed to show the type of resolve and mental toughness they showed all those years ago.

The grandfathers truly believed that Britain was still a country of great opportunities if you want to seize the chances on offer compared to where they were born. Through hard work and commitment, one can generally reach one's goals as long as they are realistic. 'If you cannot make it in Britain, you cannot make it anywhere,' said one grandfather, and many agreed with him. They were clear that if they had stayed in the Caribbean or Africa, they would not have achieved what they had in Britain. They also believe that today's generations are not as mentally strong as they were and can lack traditional family values that tie families together when facing adversity.

The pursuit of money

Without exception, the grandfathers felt that the pursuit of money always existed, but it had reached an epidemic level whereby it seems to have become the most important thing in people's lives. They talked about growing up poor but being happy with life. They do not discount that we need money to survive, otherwise they would not have travelled to the UK, but they felt that the extremes to which people will go obtain money have tilted the scales in the wrong direction over the decades. Politics and elections are about economic prosperity and stable economies rather than the health and wellbeing of the nation. The news concentrates heavily on company profit warnings, the FTSE 100, and stock markets around the world rather than human stories and endeavours. It would seem that wealth accumulation and being successful in business is held in higher regard than community involvement and volunteer work. The size of your bank account and showing off your wealth seems, at times, to be more important than a person's character. We have lost the importance of the power of the collective over individualism and the pursuit of riches. Some grandfathers spoke in an almost biblical manner, warning of the dangers of the pursuit of money becoming a way of life; a religion, for some people. These people think, live, eat, and breathe money and do not mind what they do to others in order to obtain it.

Lessons in life

The stories and advice to which I listened from all of the grandfathers I met is something we need to take on board. I do not want to give the feeling that they are perfect. On the contrary, some of them have experienced and endured every conceivable hardship known to man whilst in Britain. Also, they have made mistakes along the way, so their shared stories and advice was given to try to help us younger fathers to avoid making the same mistakes they had. The sharing of their experiences in this chapter is borne out of decades of living in Britain and being brought up in Africa and the Caribbean. They have the unique positions of having experienced different cultures and countries and in a timeframe long enough to obtain an overview of the changes that have taken place in parenting through the years. Even if you do not agree with everything they have said, I hope you will find the time to put some of their useful wisdom into practice. Or better still, if you have lost contact with uncles, aunties, or cousins, why not look them up to see how they are doing?

My Money, Your Money, Our Money

'I have enough money to last me the rest of my life unless I buy something.'
– Jackie Mason

Although this chapter is about money, it is not about how to become a millionaire or how to obtain the best savings accounts or investment portfolios. You can make an appointment to see a financial adviser or read a book to find out this type of information. This chapter is about our emotional relationships with money in our everyday lives and how our upbringing and influences in life have affected our thinking, communication, and disagreements with our partners as to how to manage and spend our money. Have you wondered how some couples seem to manage their money so good whilst other couples seem to argue about money all the time?

I had the privilege of meeting so many fathers in various financial situations, and they would like to share some of their everyday financial experiences. Hopefully, we can work out which financial models seem to work, and which do not.

The starting point

More than ever before, research shows that after infidelity, couples are either arguing or splitting up over financial disagreements. The pressure on couples to make ends meet is immense, and if you are by yourself, it is even harder. In relationships, you usually find that a person who is considered to be better with money is expected to sort out – or at least, be on top of sorting out – the finances: insurance, mortgage, rent, and the general planning of bill payments. The other partner is either less knowledgeable or just does not take responsibility for the finances and is happy to leave the organising of the finances to his/her partner. This can become tiresome for the person who is constantly juggling the family finances to ensure ends meet or carrying the impact of debt that, at times, is not of his/her making.

Patrick: 'I wasted my money as a teenager. I was living the high life, driving a BMW convertible I couldn't really afford, and buying the latest clothes and CDs. Seriously, sometimes, I lived on corned beef and dumplings to keep my BMW on the road. It was a part of my skin, my image. I didn't care, really, because I was the centre of attraction. I knew where the best raves were, and people knew that if they rolled with me, they were bound to have a good time. I'm suffering now as I have bad credit. The bad credit really affects my ability to obtain loads of stuff like a mortgage, loans, and even interest-free loans on sofas. I tried to purchase sofas for our flat as ours are very old and was turned down. It's embarrassing; can you believe it – a sofa? Ask me where all the CDs I bought are now and I couldn't tell you. As for the BMW, that was taken away by creditors when I fell behind with the payments. My past has caught up with me, and it puts a strain on our relationship, but my woman is really supportive and is helping me to resolve my bad credit history. If I'm honest, if it weren't for her, I probably would have financially gone under by now.'

Patrick's story really sets the scene for this chapter because I met and spoke with a lot of men to find out how they learned about the concept of money and how this had an impact on their behaviours and spending habits. I found three distinct attitudes towards money and how this shapes whether or not relationships are financially strained.

'My money'- man
Described as men who feel their money is for them alone.

For every financial success story I have heard, I can tell you five unsuccessful stories. I met a few fathers who either enjoyed what they considered to be 'just a-flutter on the horses or football game' or some other type of gambling like the Lotto and/or spending money on recreation (cannabis was popular) drugs. On the whole, gambling is harmless for the majority of those who participate, who see it as a fun type of irregular entertainment. However, for some fathers, gambling or other social activities, such as spending on cars and entertainment, can affect a family's finances. I met such a father who, for obvious reasons, would prefer to remain anonymous:

> **Father:** 'I knew my money was meant to go towards the washing machine and fridge-freezer – they were on their last legs – but this horse was a sure bet. All information pointed to the horse's recent good form, and I thought I couldn't lose.'

So, they agreed to save a set amount of money each month. They decided not to use their credit cards to purchase items to avoid paying interest. That was good financial management, making their money work for them rather than making interest payments to multi-national credit card companies.

However, this father did not keep to his end of the bargain as he had promised his wife. He felt a quick bet and win on the horses would mean a quicker purchase that would please everyone. His wife was unaware of his decision to take the £400 they had saved to place a bet on a horse. You see, he viewed the money they had saved as 'his money,' rather than 'their money'. The horse lost and with it went their hard-earned £400. To cap it off, he did not tell his wife he had gambled the £400 until he had finally plucked up the courage to tell her because she was pressuring him to purchase a fridge. A week later, the fridge broke down, and he had to purchase a fridge on his credit card.

Father: 'To this day, I am still paying off for the fridge due to the interest on my credit card. My wife is still fuming with me, and she accused me of being irresponsible, and she is right.'

His thought process was to risk what he saw as 'his money' without consulting his wife, who had also contributed to the savings for the fridge. His actions affected the whole family as the food in their fridge went off. Instead of thinking, 'I need to consult with my wife so that we can make a joint decision,' he decided not to and lost the money by gambling. Of course, he may have a gambling addiction, but this is difficult for me to say without further discussion. What I can say is that this is not the first time he had spent money without consulting his wife, so you can understand her anger.

Interestingly, having spoken to both grandfathers and fathers who were brought up in Africa and the Caribbean, women invariably ran the household on a daily basis, deciding what to buy for the home and what to eat. However, the men seem to make the big financial decisions like moving home or the amount available to spend on a new fridge or household repairs, with the woman deciding on the type and model. This traditional type of arrangement is not necessarily the case in Britain, where an attitude towards equality and women increasing their spending power means that they are much more involved in the financial decision-making.

In fact, quite a lot of men admitted that their partners are in charge of the household finances and are doing a much better job than they could. This attitude seems to permeate throughout relationships, whether the male is good or bad with the finances, but it does suggest the root of the financial issues sometimes lies in what we believe our role with money to be within the family.

The father who gambled was not the only father I met who had similarly spent sums of money without consulting his partner. These men tended to have the attitude that they were entitled to their money – or 'my money' – so they did not necessarily think they needed or wanted to consult with their partners when making decisions to spend. When challenged, they admitted they should have discussed their spending with their partners. However, they continued to make the same mistakes again and again in a different guise. Their attitudes and behaviours were that of 'my money' rather than 'our money', and the eventual fallout can be immeasurable, as some partners have forgiven them whilst others chose to separate.

'Your money'- woman

Described as women who feel their money is for them alone.

Of course, the shoe can also be on the other foot for men when their partners' attitudes to money can become damaging for their relationships. The area that seems to irritate men more than anything else is their wives' or partners' purchases of things they consider impractical or to have no apparent practical function, such as the tenth handbag, twentieth pair of shoes, a pair of ornaments or more towels of various sizes. Like most spending, it can be healthy within moderation, but there are many stories from the fathers of their partners' spending and refusing to change their attitudes and behaviours around spending though it places a strain on their relationships.

Interestingly, some fathers seemed to understand the importance of women buying clothes and beauty products. As the seasons and styles change on a yearly basis, the fathers felt it was inevitable that women would want to replenish their wardrobes. As one wife reminded her husband as he complained about her buying yet another top, 'Do you want me to wear the same clothes all the time? I like to look good and feel good.' Some fathers admitted to liking clothes but did not see keeping up to date with the latest fashions as important as their partners did. As fathers with competing financial pressures, we eventually slow down on our buying of the latest designer clothes for – let's say – more moderate-costing clothes to compensate for increased bills. The younger fathers did not share this view and continued to purchase brand name clothes as part of their image and sense of style. It was common for their girlfriends to shop with them and contribute their opinions on what to buy, and this was valued by the younger fathers and seen as normal behaviour.

> **Darrel:** 'We know the right clothes on our partners can make them feel and look stunning, so why interfere? The "dressing up" has long been an African and Caribbean tradition among women, and long may it continue. I like my girlfriend to come along to give her views; she knows what suits me.'

However, the persistent buying of bags, shoes, the latest cosmetics, and Internet shopping is what some men seem to find difficult to understand. Rightly or wrongly, fathers believe that once the number of items increases to the point of being unrealistic, their partners' purchases are impulse buys.

> **Tony:** 'My wife likes buying expensive handbags. I'm talking £150 plus a shot, and she now buys them online whilst at work, knowing that I am not around to comment. If I added up how many bags she has bought this year, I would faint, and that's just the ones I know about. What I don't understand is that we have utility and other bills to pay, so when I see another bag, I think that it could have gone on one of the bills. I feel she doesn't think like that; it's like the bag is calling her name, calling her to buy it.'

Of course, this is a particular father's story and his subjective view of events, as his wife may have a different viewpoint, as she was not there to give her side of the story. I wanted a balanced view on the subject, so

I spoke to a few women that I know who also loved shopping for handbags. They are clear that they work hard all week and feel that with their hard-earned cash, they should be able to indulge in rewarding themselves with a few gifts. They were clear that their husbands' views on their spending might differ from their viewpoints. Their husbands looked at the handbags to decide whether they had functional values, and if they could not place a function on the bag, they viewed them as worthless and saw one bag as good as another. What men fail to understand is that bags are a fashion accessory, but they also carry a woman's necessities, which is something to which men cannot relate.

You can see how his wife's attitude towards money can be viewed as 'your money' rather than 'our money' as he feels that she is placing her desire to purchase her handbags above the family's bills and other financial commitments. The feeling of not being able to stop or influence your partner's spending habits can make both men and women feel powerless to try to come to a common financial agreement. The arguments ended up being about apportioning blame when it came to spending habits, rather than both sides admitting to wanting autonomy to spend as they saw fit. However, without a formula for tackling their financial attitudes and behavioural differences, these couples ended up breaking up due to unresolved and irrevocable financial difficulties.

'Our money'

A couple wanted to plan a family getaway during the summer holidays. At dinnertime, they narrowed their choices to either Spain or the more expensive Disney World in Florida. They decided on Florida, but this would take extra discipline and effort to save. Mum and Dad agreed to open a holiday savings account and save a set amount each month in order to reach their holiday target.

Their 12- and 16-year-old children cleaned neighbours' cars and sold fizzy drinks on the weekend, and all proceeds went into the holiday fund. They reached their target in 12 months, rather than the planned 18 and were on a plane to Florida with two children for an all-inclusive holiday. The couple said it was the best holiday they'd ever had, especially knowing they came home debt-free with no credit card bills. The children also loved and valued the holiday more because they had earned it through their hard work.

> **Philip:** 'We have continued with our holiday account. Our son is working now and contributes to the account on a monthly basis. Not all of our holidays are as expensive as Florida, but we do get to go away together on a regular basis. Having a financial plan not only for our holidays but also for our shopping, bill payments, and savings plans have really worked for us. The challenge is keeping to the plan and when you...derail, it's important to get straight back to the goals you have set.'

This couple seemed to understand the importance of financial planning and setting achievable goals with their family. I met other fathers who had various financial planning and savings with their partners. What struck me was that they were in the minority. In general, they seemed less emotional whilst discussing money and had fewer arguments with their wives about money. The reason it would seem is that their financial planning, communication around money, and most importantly, the way they have set up their bank accounts minimised the arguments. Curious? Well, read on, and I will explain.

Joint Accounts

With the increase in women working and having financial independence from their husbands, joint income households have become much more common, and it seems to make sense to have joint accounts to pay the rent and/or mortgage and other household bills. The actual amount men and women agree to contribute varies depending on who earns more. For instance, if the woman earns more per month, she might contribute more than the man and vice versa. I am informed that this arrangement is based on trust, so debts are paid on time. The trust is built on coming to an agreement and sticking to the monthly amount you pay into the joint account to cover the monthly payments.

Payments into joint accounts may be used to cover utility bills, council taxes, water, telephone, TV, and rent and/or mortgage. You do not have to pay all of your bills this way; you may choose to leave some as quarterly payments to spread the payments throughout the year. Of course, if you are old school, and you would like the bill to hit your doorstep, you can continue to do so, but fathers do not believe that this is a very economical way of paying the bills as companies now give incentive discounts for direct debit payments throughout the year.

For the joint accounts to work honestly with your partners, it is absolutely crucial to counter any difficulties that may arise. For instance, if you are short of money and lower your contribution to the joint account and do not inform your partners, you may miss the direct debit payments and incur late fees.

> **Joseph:** 'Communication is vital, and to avoid any mishaps and arguments, I find it better to set up a monthly direct debit payment into our joint account for a day after I am paid. It means that I do not have to worry about not having money to pay the rent, and it forces you to budget the remainder of your money to last the month.'

Setting up a joint account with your partner is easy to do. In fact, this process is the easiest part of the financial arrangement. The majority of fathers to whom I spoke thought joint accounts were a good idea, but that didn't mean they would all fly out the door to do it. There seems to be some reluctance regarding the fathers' 'my money' psychology that makes them feel uncomfortable with such arrangements. In particular, male-breadwinner households in which men are used to controlling the finances found the joint account concept more difficult to accept, but these were in the minority.

There are advantages to having joint accounts that answer our questions about maintaining happy homes. The couples with joint accounts also have their own current accounts, and there is a clear agreement between these couples. Once the agreed-upon amount of money has been transferred into their joint accounts to cover their financial commitments, the remainder of the money in their separate current accounts is theirs to do with as they please.

> **Bartholomew:** 'We find our joint account and our own accounts work...really well because we have different tastes, and if all of our money was tied up in our joint account, and I wanted to buy a new digital camera, and she wanted to buy a pair of boots, we would argue over whose need was the greatest. We like it this way.'

Listening to all the fathers with joint accounts and their reasoning behind them provides us with an efficient and effective way of communicating with our partners and/or wives and managing our families' finances. This method combines financial accountability on both sides and a sense of independence with separate accounts for buying the things they want without it leading to arguments. So, guys, with your leftover money, you can buy the latest gadgets without having to justify your purchases, and the same would apply to your partners.

'My money', 'your money' – a house divided

Whether it is the man or the woman who spends money without due regard for the impact on the family or their relationship, this is a major reason why some couples separate. Individual or secretive spending outside of people's partners' consent can cause a lot of resentment between couples, as one invariably has to ensure the books balance at the end of the month.

I have found that money disagreements are a symptom of a wider problem within relationships. Yes, in some relationships, there exists a real difference in the attitudes towards spending and money, but the real cause is a breakdown in communication between couples, and money problems just amplify the situation. For instance, we, as men, are known for our lack of patience or 'turning off' when our partners want to have meaningful conversations. A few fathers admitted to not liking being questioned about how they spend. Blame then becomes commonplace, rather than looking for solutions that suit both parties, like deciding on a time at which both parties can talk to solve the problem.

From my journey around the country, I have found that the couples who are not in sync and who view their money separately are the least satisfied with their financial arrangements with their partners. They seem to be living together but not making important financial decisions together and on a regular basis. There tends to be a general difficulty in communication, and finances have a way of bringing this to a boil.

The couples that communicate and share joint responsibility – or at least agree on how to organise their finances around their strengths and weaknesses – are less stressed about the next bill as they seem to have control, and they experience fewer financial surprises. They tend to share the same dreams and work towards obtaining their goals together. For instance, some fathers spoke about buying a house together, and they are well on their way to realising this dream because both sides have a common goal, and they are making financial sacrifices to realise their dream.

The question is: how do mere mortals like us obtain this equilibrium with our partners to maintain a sense of financial independence, allowing us to buy things or pursue our hobbies without causing almighty arguments with our wives and vice versa? One of the fatherhood groups discussed some really good ideas to solve our dilemma, and I would like to share some of them with you.

The 'one account' couple – Is this the future?

Here is another idea, but it is not for the faint-hearted. During a discussion on finances, one father explained that he shares one current and one savings account with his wife, and they do not have separate accounts of their own. All of their disposable income goes into their one account, which also pays their bills.

Some fathers in the group were genuinely surprised and intrigued to find out how this setup worked, and they asked questions for clarification.

> **Father 1**: 'How do you avoid arguments as men and women tend to have separate spending habits? Don't tell me there are no arguments over spending.'

> **One account father**: 'Sharing one account has made us more responsible spenders. You only tend to buy the things you need rather than the things you desire.'

> **Father 2**: 'And you are okay with this arrangement?'

The other fathers were surprised that he and his wife did not feel they needed some type of financial independence, but the 'one account' father held his ground and explained:

> **One account father**: 'Financial decisions on spending are made by both of us, and if I wanted to buy something, I would discuss it with my wife. I do not feel the need to control our finances, and trust is a big factor in our decision to have just the one account. We both spend far less than we would do if we had separate accounts. I strongly recommend one account to everyone because it's the ultimate in trust.'

As I looked around the room at the other fathers, they were still thinking about his confident assertion that having just one account is the way forward for couples. One father still seemed sceptical, and this showed in the questions he asked him.

> **Father 3**: 'So, for all you know, your wife might be siphoning money into another account for a rainy day, and you wouldn't even know about it. She could have a nest egg in case things don't work out, and you wouldn't even know, or she – or you – could be overspending and vice versa.'

> **One account father**: 'Yeah, but I trust my wife. I'm not being naïve – we have an expectation of each other to be responsible adults and not take advantage. Also, there are other checks and counterbalances that can be made as we both receive bank statements. So, just because I do not always check the statements, it does not mean I cannot at a later date if I choose to.'

One account between couples was a new concept for the fathers and myself. The majority of fathers felt they would have to ask a lot more fathers to see if anyone else had this arrangement to gauge its success. What is clear is that the one account idea is new, fresh, dynamic, and built on trust. It certainly gave all of us food for thought as to whether this will be the way of the future or just an idea that will never catch on.

Financial literacy

For those fathers who struggle with the concept of joint accounts because they are so used to having their own separate accounts, this section may help.

In his book, *Rich Dad Poor Dad*, Robert Kiyosaki explains the concept of financial literacy. Financial literacy is about how you – as an individual or with your partner – treat your hard-earned money. It is about what you do with your money every month you receive a paycheque. It is about whether you have developed bad spending habits that make it hard for you to account for your money or if you see any concrete benefits. It is about how you make your money work for you rather than against you. It is about what you do as a family in your home to minimise your spending and maximise your income.

I hope you can apply some of his ideas about financial literacy to our families' lives to benefit us all. Money is not just about how much money you make but how much money you keep. There are many stories of lottery winners who end up being poor again or famous footballers earning millions at the height of their careers only to claim social security when their careers end. A part of financial literacy is taking the emotional attachment out of money. As Kiyosaki puts it, 'If your pattern in life is to spend everything you get, most likely an increase in cash will just result in an increase in spending.'

Thinking more practically about how you can manage your money better to allow your and your families' dreams to become a reality must be our ultimate goals rather than struggling to make ends meet every month. We need to get away from trying to keep up with our neighbours and friends and going along with the crowd because loans, credit cards, and other financial inducements are how we get ourselves into financial messes. It's not financially literate to continue in this vein, but we do.

The fact is that money can be fun, but we have to learn to take some of our hard-earned cash and regularly either save or invest. Rich people call this investment 'asset building' (owning businesses, stocks, shares, royalties, investments, and savings), whereby they are able to earn a passive income from their assets. They reward themselves in the future by looking for ways to make money by not having to be at a given place to do so. For instance, I met a father who decided to hire out his driveway to a working woman who needed to park her car safely near a station to commute to work. This father was earning money without having to be there; this is what is called passive income. From this passive income, this father can either purchase items without having to obtain a loan or use his credit card; he can add the money to his savings or reinvest it in his assets. We use credit or loans to buy the things we want and pay the added interest charges to 'borrow' the money because no one has taught us about financial literacy.

Of course, financial literacy is not just about short-term goals but also long-term goal setting with your family in mind. Because we live and work in such a fast-paced world, how often do we sit and discuss our finances with our partners to ensure we are pulling in the same direction? The example of the family who went on holiday and used the 'our money' approach was a start, and you can apply this to any situation with your family. From energy-saving ideas to asset-building portfolios, nothing is beyond our reach.

Separated fathers stuck in the 'my money' loop

Another group of fathers we have not touched on are those separated from their partners but still have financial responsibilities towards their children. They were in the minority, but they were sizeable, nevertheless. Interestingly, finance seemed to be a central factor (but not the only reason) as to why they had separated from their partners, so it fits nicely into this chapter. These fathers admitted that, as a couple, there was little consensus on their financial planning, and although they were no longer together, these arguments have continued, especially when large debts were hidden.

Quite rightly, there is a lot written in the media about men who do not financially support their children and the social and financial impact this causes. I have met some of these fathers on my travels, and it always amazes me how these fathers try to justify their actions – or should I say, non-action. Some of these men are seriously 'vexed' for one reason or another and find it difficult to separate their feelings about their ex-partners from the financial needs of their children. They are caring fathers in the sense that they see their children (though the amount of contact varied), but the tension with their ex-partners can make communication difficult and financial arrangements precarious.

A classic example I came across time and time again were disputes with their ex-partners over their financial contribution towards the children and differences on what they feel their children actually needed bought for them.

For instance, a few fathers said they felt their children needed a coat or shoes, so they brought it rather than communicate their intentions or give the money to their ex-partners to buy the items. This action caused tension between parties because their ex-partners had already bought the clothes needed for their children. The rights and wrongs of these fathers' approaches are not for us to judge, as we are all human and fallible in some way. It would seem that if there was an amicable break-up, the financial negotiations seemed to flow quite smoothly, and some type of trust existed that allowed both parents to make joint decisions. These decisions took place over phone calls but mainly text messages with respect to what was needed for the children, who would purchase what, or what each parent would contribute towards the items.

Unfortunately, not all relationships are so amicable, and this is usually due to unresolved issues leaving tension between ex-partners when they separate. The reason I say unresolved is because rather than talk about financial issues, they tended to talk about why they'd separated, difficulties they were having with their ex-partners over access, or feeling that new boyfriends were unduly influencing their children. As you can imagine, such emotive issues usually spilt into arguments and accusations of unreasonable demands and mistrust on both sides as to financial needs for the children. Some fathers openly admitted to finding it hard to give money to their ex-partners at times, preferring to purchase items for the children as a means of control.

However, there are separated men who are doing the right thing by supporting their families, and they do not seem so wrapped up in the past, having 'let go' in order to move on with their lives. Some of these men have less disposable income due to their living outside of the family home and still contributing towards it. For them, money is at a premium, and financial priorities need to be focused and can, at times, lead to financial hardship, so tough financial decisions have to be made along the way.

The fathers who are serious about supporting their children emotionally, practically, and financially know that times for them will be hard, but they are willing to muddle through because they know it won't be forever. These fathers had less sympathy for the fathers who were unwilling to sacrifice and tended to give excuses for not doing as much as they should for their children financially. Ironically, the fathers who were in disagreement with their ex-wives saw these fathers as being push-overs or soft, pandering to the wishes of their exes and giving in to have a quiet life. Wow!

Finding a system that works for all

As mentioned earlier, some separated fathers eventually worked out systems that seemed to work for them, and they shared their experiences with other fathers. They became tired of the constant financial battles and wanted to resolve and build amicable financial relationships with their ex-partners for the sake of their children and their sanity. Finding a middle ground and letting go of past issues and arguments has led to less tension with their ex-partners in the long run.

What seemed to work for these men was to view the communication and contact with their ex-partners almost like a business relationship, where past problems were left out of the decisions for finances and access to care as no one prospers when ill feelings are the main guests.

They suggest starting a dialogue with ex-wives based on mutual respect. There was also an acknowledgement that there are women who make things difficult for the fathers by winding them up or using the children to 'get back' at them. However, we can only be responsible for our own actions and not what others do or say. Again, the message from the fathers who have cracked the communication difficulties is to be business-like in given situations. If you do not fan the flames of past arguments, then eventually, there will be nothing for you and your ex to argue about. Do what is right for your children by being in their lives and taking some of the immense burdens from the mothers for caring for the children. As one father put it, "Children are for life, so be a man and stop arguing."

Educating your children around the 'our money' concept

Do you or your partner have a singular 'my money' approach, or do you have a joint approach to money where it is seen as 'our money', and you both take responsibility for juggling the finances to make ends meet? Whether you have a positive or negative attitude towards money management, your children will be influenced by you and are likely to follow in your footsteps.

You only have to listen to the news or open a newspaper to read that the UK is the European capital of credit card debt. We have become a nation of buy-first-pay-later. Since the deregulation of the financial service in the early 1990s, we've been bombarded by financial services, offering what seemed to be mouth-watering credit and loan deals. The increase in our spending power led to the showing off of our perceived wealth to others. The creation of the 'Buppie' and 'Yuppie' personified the image of greed and individuality. The 'showing off' of one's wealth became commonplace, leading, at times, to individuality and competition becoming more important than community and cooperation. The modern-day entrepreneurs are influencers and vloggers who do not hesitate to flaunt their wealth on social media. Or should I say so-called wealth, as we are now aware that some of them borrow cars and designer clothes, to give the impression that they are rich. The impact on the young can be psychologically damaging, as they aspire to have the same, to be rich. Both young and old can be seduced by the lure of wanting to emulate these Influencers. But are unaware of all the unsuccessful stories and the traumatic financial bankruptcy for those who do not succeed.

The attitude towards money was to spend now and save later, and a lot of people and families are feeling the aftermath of years of excess spending, living beyond their means, and having to pay the money back to credit card companies now, money that was never theirs in the first place. If you were to ask your parents, we know what they would say about the UK's credit card spending.

In contrast, our parents warned us of the dangers of spending what we do not have and tried to teach us to save for the things we need and not want. Being low wage earners moulded their attitudes towards money, and the lack of borrowing from banks necessitated the need for interdependency in the community and the development of a community financial saving system called 'Partner', which eventually led to the modern-day Credit Unions. In the chapter **Back to the Future – Grandfathers Speak**, the importance of the partner in ensuring that large appliances were affordable cannot be understated, but there was also a sense that they were saving for their families back home, so sending money back home was very popular and followed the tradition of 'our money'. As the old saying goes, 'To give is to receive'. The save for a rainy-day attitude was strong because they did not feel they had job security and wanted some savings to fall back on in times of need.

So, although on the whole, we grew up being influenced by our parents, somewhere along the way we were seduced by the advertising and forgot the important lesson that money is not about 'my money' or 'your money' but 'our money' that ensures the family grows and prospers, and not to the determent of the family.

When I first became a father, I met an African American father on holiday. He told me that he and his friends had given their children two books as a gift. The preferred books centred around Martin Luther King and another one on basic financial planning. The first book was to understand the importance of our history and the tolerance of a great man in a time of intolerance. The second book was to teach their children the importance of financial planning, as this was a lifelong education. These American fathers believed that with the proper guidance, their children would learn the importance and practice of sound financial planning at an early age, as well as to learn how not to hate yourself or others and to embrace humanity no matter what colour or culture people are from. They have a point.

What all these examples show is that if we pull together as a family, we will become more effective at looking after 'our money'. The 'my money'/'your money' mentality can be strong in both males and females.

However, it usually starts and finishes in a non-focused financial type of existence that lacks commitment towards the future of your bank balance and communication between couples. The good news is that the more fathers talk to each other and share their experiences and knowledge, the better practical understanding our families will gain. So, financial literacy is not a mathematical equation that is hard to understand or learn.

As with most things in life, our children learn from us, so if we teach our children to have goals and learn financial literacy and support them, the concept of 'our money' rather than 'my money' will develop within.

So, I Hear Your Woman Earns More Than You!

"Equality will be achieved when men and women are granted equal pay and equal respect."

– Beyoncé

Changing work trends between men and women

This topic caused the most controversy within one fatherhood group I facilitated. Finding fathers who were prepared to discuss their earnings proved initially difficult. At one stage, I thought my pursuit of this topic might lead to some members of the group voting with their feet. Discussions about earnings can become contentious at the best of times, but add trying to discuss the fact that some women now earn more than their male partners to the mix, and you have a dangerous cocktail for arguments that can explode at any time.

So, here are the stories of fathers who struggled to deal with this sensitive issue. Some of their comments may not be to everyone's liking, and I apologise for this in advance. I hope our beautiful sisters do not take offence, as we do not mean to disrespect you – it is clear that your view on the subject is not covered in this chapter – but in the heat of the moment, their stories provide us with powerful illustrations of some men's difficulty with a changing world and the psychological fight they go through to rationalise the past with the present.

At long last, women are coming more and more to the forefront in the world of work in different professions. I have four sisters, and I welcome their talents finally being acknowledged in the world of work. My mother's generation did not have the same opportunities as today's women. Mum, with her evolving women's rights attitude, and my sisters are quite clear that women should not be held back in any walk of life due to their gender. The fact is that, in our changing world, women – and especially women of colour – continue to face discrimination over equal pay compared to their male counterparts. The trend is that some women are becoming more financially independent and gaining more control over their lives and destinies. This poses an interesting dilemma for some men whose masculinity and self-esteem are based on being the main breadwinner in the family, and they feel their purpose in life may be in jeopardy if women continue to excel.

Interestingly, a major study by the Joseph Rowntree Foundation goes against the prevailing statistical evidence that the male breadwinner is dying out. The research found that, in areas where families of Pakistani, Caribbean, and African backgrounds reside, the stereotypical breadwinner model is still prevalent. Despite the increase of mothers who work, the prevailing attitude between both parents and children is that a father's stereotypical role is to earn money and protect the family. In particular, fathers view their roles as financial providers as a key part of their identities and major contributors to their sense of worth.

Research on earning tension between sexes

A study based on government research carried out by the think tank Future Foundation (2007) concluded that by 2030 40% of women would earn more than men, compared to the present figure of 14%. Women's income has historically been affected by their decision to stay at home to look after their families. The researchers identified that 2020 would be the year the shift in power would start with women taking more responsibility for family budgets. The study found that 27% of today's 16-24-year-old women would prefer to be the main breadwinners. The fact that females obtain higher educational qualifications than their male counterparts could also lead to women overtaking men on the wage front in the future. Future Foundation concluded that, as women's contributions to the household income grow, they will take on greater responsibility in financial decisions relating to the home. Fifty years ago, financial decisions tended to be the exclusive domain of men. *The Guardian Newspaper* (2006) highlighted a Skipton Building Society survey that found that just over a fifth of the women surveyed said the financial imbalance within their relationships sparked rows. Among the men who earned less than their female partners, one in seven felt 'stripped' of their financial independence, which supports the Joseph Rowntree Research whereby some of the sampling of men felt that earning was their role within the family.

'Now that women's earning power has changed, deeply held beliefs about male- female roles and financial responsibility...can cause anger and resentment... this can often lead to rows.'

– Christine Northam, Relate Family counsellor (2006)

Is this the end of the fatherhood group?

The research seems to back up the fact that some men have the attitude of holding onto their families' financial responsibilities. However, changes are on the horizon, and some men struggle to accept this. The topic of women earning more than men surfaced a few times whilst talking about other financial issues (joint bank accounts, spending habits of men and women), but moved quickly on after comments such as, 'Well, I earn more than my woman,' or 'I make the decisions around finance,' or the more measured response, 'We talk about things, and we make joint decisions.' I was grappling with whether this was their reality or comments the fathers had become accustomed to saying when amongst other males. They were strong statements that would ensure their traditional breadwinner status and remain unchallenged within the group. The more I tried to open up a discussion on men and women's earning, the more I sensed avoidance from the group. For instance, one father said, 'That topic is dead in the water, bruv,' and 'What do you want to know about that for? I'm providing for my family.' The fatherhood group was giving me the clear message that they did not want to discuss this topic further, but it was too late.

The stubborn defence of their positions added to the research findings fuelled my intrigue and pushed me to want to explore the topic further. I sensed that although they were initially reluctant, they were, in essence, an expressive and responsive group. Just because the topic was viewed by some as taboo because it struck at the heart of some men's existences, that would not deter me from asking uncomfortable questions.

A part of the underlying difficulty this particular group experienced centred around two regular members' attendance decreasing, and no one seemed to know why. In fact, the general membership had started to fall slightly, and one father approached me after a session to explain why: some fathers were uncomfortable talking about earnings within the group. He explained that Desmond (a father) had felt uncomfortable because his partner earned more than him, and although he loved coming to the group, he would only return when the 'heat' had died down on the subject.

I contacted Desmond, and he shared his reservations with me, but what he failed to realise was that his absence, along with the others, had an effect on the group, who felt they had let them down in some way. Desmond felt a sense of relief that he had shared his situation with me and came to realise that by isolating himself from the group, he had isolated himself from the support the group had to offer. After all, that was the reason they all attended: to build up a support system and share ideas on the relationships and thier parenting experience.

I contacted a close friend of mine. He is an extremely educated, intelligent, calm, and analytical person. Interestingly, his wife earns more than him, and I wanted to find out how he dealt with it and whether he could support me when introducing the topic to the group. His story and insight were fascinating. When he first dated his wife, he earned more than her. He was already working, and she was training to be a solicitor. As time passed, they married, had children, and before he realised, she was earning nearly double his income. The change in their income dynamics really affected him. He had been brought up in a traditional, male breadwinner family model, and the gender roles within his family were set. Of course, you had women who crossed over into the work sphere, but they tended to occupy part-time, low positions and earnings. Their income was seen as 'extra' to help the family out.

He had been programmed from an early age to provide for his family. He did not mind his wife working as times had changed, and it is commonplace for women to have a career. In fact, he knew she was intelligent and destined for a successful career, and he supported her during university, but for his wife to earn nearly double his income – well, this really rattled his manhood and his perspective on the roles within his family.

I asked him how he had overcome his feelings and how could I broach the subject with the group without deathly silence hitting the room. He humorously reminded me of his uncle's favourite saying: 'You can take the man out of the country, but you cannot take the country out of the man.' So, some members of the fatherhood group would never be able to get past the need to earn more than their partners. Their homes are based on the traditional breadwinner model, and a part of their existence as the male is based on the status quo, so no amount of talking would change their attitudes.

He explained his turmoil and scattered thought process at the initial changes in his wife's income: 'I thought, for so long, I was the breadwinner, so shouldn't I still be earning more than her? When I think about it, I was more bothered about what my male friends would say if they found out.' He identified a few of his male friends who ribbed him with comments like 'Who really wears the trousers in your house then?' He eventually realised that his wife's earning more than him did not conform to how he expected providing for his family to be. He realised that his wife was not the problem – he was, and his silly comments and rows were due to the frustration he felt, which had started to have an impact on their marriage. Something had to be done and fast.

Through a lot of soul searching and talking to some friends, he realised what a wonderful life he has. The good quality of life his family experienced was down to two hard-working parents who were very much in love and committed to their family. He needed to stop concentrating on money alone and realise that money was not his or hers but theirs. This was similar to the 'my money', 'your money', 'our money' chapter that highlighted the importance of having a joint financial plan rather than a selfish attitude when it came to money accumulation. His wife knew that he was finding the transition difficult, and she helped him through the period, hanging in there for her man.

With my new-found understanding and sensitivity of the issue, I took the topic back to the fatherhood group, and rather than start cold with the topic of money, I took a step back and explained, statistically, the pressure on relationships due to financial changes and pressures this was bound to cause. My friend attended the group to talk about his experience. The group was intrigued to meet him, and comments prior to the meeting from fathers included:

'That's cool if he wants to talk to us.'

'He doesn't know us, and he wants to talk about his business. He's brave...or stupid.'

'That's interesting. Let's see how he copes standing in front of us.'

'He's mad. He must be mad.'

Our guest speaker

The group accepted Desmond back with open arms. The moment was touching, and our guest speaker had arrived, too. The evening was about to get very interesting. I remember closing my eyes for a split second, thinking, please, let this evening pass without a major bust-up between fathers, as I was unsure if they were ready for such a topic. For the first time, I was genuinely concerned that the group may not recover if it went badly wrong and friendships were broken as a result of my selfish reasons for wanting this topic to go ahead. As I sat waiting for my friend to organise his papers, I realised I was asking the fathers to take a huge leap of faith, to talk about a very personal issue that linked to some their very existence as males.

My friend introduced himself and explained his thoughts around money and his financial life's education, how money circulated around the economy with its ownership changing hands every day and linking this to his personal situation. He explained his initial feelings as a male earning less than his wife and how he had to overcome this by letting go of his male territorial instinct around money and understanding the cash flow within the family. He talked about starting to enjoy the benefits of having a joint-income family, irrelevant of who was earning more. It was a masterful introduction.

My friend was right. This approach meant the group did not have to directly address their situations, and it would allow the topic to be eased in via his experience. The fact is that the group had mixed feelings about his attendance, but they wanted to meet him out of curiosity, and he had caught the group's attention. As I looked around the room, there was not a single father who was not listening intensely. He had a calm charisma about him, and he spoke with experience and style that you couldn't help but respect and listen to as his journey through denial, through rage to acceptance of his situation shone through. Of course, there were awkward comments to respond to from some of our, let's say, direct fathers, such as: 'How do you really feel about your wife earning more than you?' 'You're brave to share this with guys you don't know,' and 'Just how much more money are we talking about here?'

Some of the group helped my friend, as some of the questions were personal. Commendably, my friend decided to answer some but not all of the questions. Some fathers liked his rational way of working through his issues and could relate to his experience. Desmond proved to be the star of the show, admitting that he had also faced the same issues as my friend. Having another person who understood his plight seemed to give Desmond strength, and his confidence returned to the point of his advocating for men to understand that the world was changing, and if men did not change, a lot of families could end up either under immense strain through constant arguing or breaking up. There was stunned silence around the room as everyone waited for someone to say something – anything – but no one did apart from my friend. He explained that feelings are very subjective, and this issue will affect men in different ways, but the insightful message he had given the group was that more and more of his male friends were open and proud about their partners earning more than them. At some stage in their lives, men are likely to have to face up to their partners being more educated and earning more than them.

The evening was a success, as the fathers crowded around my friend, either to thank him for attending and sharing his experience or to further quiz him to see if he was for real. What of Desmond? Well, he's fine, and facilitates small groups on emotionally coming to terms with financial changes between couples.

Coping with a changing world

Although the Joseph Rowntree Foundation study highlighted that the male breadwinner model is still evident in our communities, we cannot discount the fact that by 2030, 40% of women will earn more than men. As men, we have to be prepared for this change rather than fear this shift in the workplace and at home. With my friend's assistance, this fatherhood group drew up a list of 'into the unknown' that we, as men, will have to work through to understand the changes that might happen in our households one day to be prepared for the changes.

1. Your partner wanting to improve herself does not mean she wants to leave you. She wants to improve the quality of life you have together for everyone's wellbeing and happiness.

2. Earning more than your wife does not have to be linked to your masculinity, and her earning more than you does not have to be linked to your lack of masculinity.

3. If you feel threatened, embarrassed, angry, or confused by your wife's earning more than you, try to be honest with yourself and identify the reasons for this. Talk to friends in a similar situation to find out how they overcame it.

4. As men, we can be very territorial about money as this leads to the ability to control the household in many ways. Joint accounts ensure the money is seen as the family's rather than any one individual. In other words, 'our money' rather than 'your money'.

5. Some male friends will rib you if your partner earns more than you, especially if they sense it really bothers you. But while your friends are at home in cold Britain, you can enjoy that extra holiday, or when your partner buys you that something you've always wanted, who will be laughing then?

6. If your wife is happy, you should enjoy the fruits of her labour and more.

7. A strong man does not have to be an ignorant man. Remember that you can take the man out of the country, but you can't take the country out of the man. Arguing over your dented ego is a sure way to spoil a beautiful relationship.

8. Accept that the opportunities for women to grow and develop in education and the workplace have never been greater, and this is likely to continue for some time to come.

9. Your partner, if she has not already done so, will want to experience new challenges as you did whilst at college, training, or work. If the tables were turned, she would support you, so you should support her.

10. Talk to her about your feelings as women invariably respond to talking and can support you in times of need.

In the group are families going through a form of metamorphosis. Due to changing times in the work sector, doors that were originally closed to women have opened up. These extraordinarily talented women in high-positioned jobs are some of the group's wives. As men, we need to leave the countryside attitude in the country, metaphorically speaking, move with the times, and accept that some women achieve pay equality and respect from society, and they deserve the same respect and support they would not hesitate to give to us.

To Read Or Not To Read With Your Children, That Is the Question.

Should fathers read with their children?

Does it matter or make a difference whether you read to with or with your children? Do you have the time or the energy to read after a long stressful day at work? Do you enjoy reading with your children, or is it a chore?

Well, the good news is that we are not going to lecture you. You don't have to read with your children if you don't want to. The education department – or the government, for that matter – have not made reading with your children at home compulsory. It is unlikely that an education welfare officer will come knocking on your door to complain that you need to read more to them, so relax at home, put your feet up, and enjoy your home comforts.

You may be wondering: hold on – what's the catch? Why such a laid-back attitude compared to some of the serious issues we men have discussed throughout this book?

Fathers totally understand how important education is for our children's future life chances and opportunities for social mobility and avoiding poverty, not to mention structural inequalities that are likely to shackle their progress at some point in their lives in this modern technological and global world in which we live. They also know that their children will need multiple and even higher qualifications just to get an interview for a job. We hear this all the time, message after message informing us that Black boys and working-class white boys struggle compared to females from all cultures, including our daughters, who are excelling in educational attainment. So, why do we need a chapter to discuss what we already know?

Well, not all of our children are thriving where education is concerned, and of course, there are many reasons for this, but what struck me was that not all, but a sizeable amount of fathers did not see the relevance or the link between reading with and to their children at a young age and their children developing a love of books and attaining a successful journey through the education system. These fathers tended to leave the educating of their children to school, the women in their family network, and even nephews and nieces. They expected their children to eventually attend school, pass their exams with flying colours, progress into university, and then obtain a top company job or a position in a successful trade.

So, although we have the majority decision amongst fathers on the importance of education, it was near impossible to get a consensus on their participation or contribution through reading to their children pre-secondary school. A major impact seems to be the fathers' own school experiences, their negative or positive relationships with teachers, and whether they felt the school cared about their futures. All of this had a great impact on their attitudes, confidence, and approach to participating in their children's education.

The fact is some fathers do not enjoy reading with their children whilst others love it as they see the link between reading standards and their participation. So, rather than spend time trying to crush each other into submission, some fathers spent time at home looking at the research, discussing whether we agreed with the findings, and the obstacles we felt contributed to our being able to read with our children. Hopefully, the following studies and our post-discussion will allow you to answer the question posed at the beginning of this chapter.

Research findings – in support of fathers reading

1. The National Literacy Trust 2020

Alison David's article debates that there can be few things as powerful as regularly reading to a young child. It has astonishing benefits for children: comfort and reassurance, confidence and security, relaxation, happiness, and fun. Giving a child time and full attention when reading them a story tells them they matter. It builds self-esteem, vocabulary, feeds the imagination, and even improves their sleeping patterns. Yet fewer than half of new-born's to two-year-olds are read to every day – or nearly every day – by their parents.

David states that regularly reading to a child for the love of it provides a connection between parent and child from the very early days and helps build strong family ties as lines from favourite stories enter the family lexicon. Families who enjoy reading together have more opportunities for discussion and develop empathy and attachment. Reading to their infants is one of the greatest gifts parents can give. By starting the journey of building a lifelong love of reading for pleasure, parents are giving their children the opportunity to be the best they can be: children who read for pleasure do better in a wide range of subjects at school, and it also positively impacts children's wellbeing.

David concludes that parents, as a wide cohort, have typically not been explicitly told about the importance of reading aloud to their child, the benefits of relaxation, time together, and the importance of building a routine and love of reading.

2. Murdoch Children's Research Institute (2018)
This research highlighted how children's language development is influenced by their fathers' involvement.

Despite the recognised importance of the home environment in promoting child development, there has been very limited longitudinal research examining the role of fathers in promoting language and literacy development. The findings remained even after taking into consideration parent income, employment, and education levels, as well as mothers' reading practices.

This suggests that fathers have a unique contribution to make to their children's language development through reading interactions. This may be because parents in the same household read the same books, but the different ways in which they read has further helped child language development, such as the way they focus on different words, pronounce things differently, or emphasise different parts of the story. All of these differences help children understand the different ways they can use language.

There is some research suggesting that fathers are more likely to scaffold children's reading, which means they divide the reading into smaller sections to enable the child to better understand the sections. However, mothers can also do this, so further studies observing parents reading to understand what the differences are, if any, are needed.

Fathers are an important part of families, and wider research suggests that getting all adults involved in children's reading can enhance their development. At present, programs are not targeted at fathers to enable them to gain the understanding and skills required to conduct high-quality reading interactions with their children.

3. The National Literacy Trust Study (2009)

Parents with lower literacy levels often lack the confidence to help their children with reading and writing, which reinforces the cycle of disadvantage. For many parents, the school curriculum is an alienating and complex framework, but strong literacy skills are the result of a partnership between parents and our education system. Supporting literacy at home can break down barriers to achievement; parental behaviour that supports their children's learning is a more powerful force for academic success than a child's socio-economic background.

4. The Institute of Education (IOE - 2013)

The research was conducted by Dr Alice Sullivan and Matt Brown, who analysed the reading behaviour of approximately 6,000 young people. The IOE's Centre for Longitudinal Studies compared children from the same social backgrounds who had achieved the same test scores at ages five and ten. They discovered that those who read books often at age ten and more than once a week at age 16 gained higher results in all three tests at age 16 than those who read less regularly.

Reading for pleasure was found to be more important for children's cognitive development between the ages 10-16 than their parents' level of education. The combined effect on children's progress when reading books often, going to the library regularly, and reading newspapers at 16 was four times greater than the advantage children gained from having a parent with a degree.

Children who were read to regularly by their parents at age five performed better in all three tests at age 16 than those who were not helped in this way. The study underlines the importance of encouraging children to read – even in the digital age. There are concerns that young people's reading for pleasure has declined. There could be various reasons for this, including more time spent in organised activities, more homework, and of course, more time spent online. However, new technologies, such as e-readers, can offer easy access to books and newspapers, and it is important that government policies support and encourage children's reading, particularly in their teenage years.

5. Top 10 Trends in Reading and Book Apps for Children – in feature articles by Porter Anderson, 2 February 2017

Apps for children and teens will continue to focus on 'enriched content', taking advantage of technical functions such as animation, interactivity, and gamification. The goal, in these cases, is to explore new storytelling approaches.

Beyond monitoring and parental control, developers are incorporating options to help parents and kids consume content together. A good example is Samsung's *Bedtime VR Stories*, so we will see more developments reinforcing this trend. Until now, most developers have chosen Apple to launch their work, and Android users haven't enjoyed the same level of attention, either in amount or content quality. However, developers prefer Android, and sales figures seem to be driving the creation of more Android apps for children and young adults.

For parents or teachers, viewing and/or access control can be useful when the goal is to monitor the use of an app to follow a user's progress and provide support.

Research as opposed to fathers reading to their children
We could not find any!

Fathers' responses to the studies
Every father to whom I spoke with agreed that education for their children was of prime importance. Attendance at school and/or college was a must, and application to their studies was a high expectation.

However, looking at the studies and discussing their findings together provided varying attitudes and approaches to the issues of reading with their children. Some fathers believed the studies placed too much importance on fathers who read with their children would lead to success at school. They believed that many factors contributed to success at school and/or college, such as visiting libraries with their children, watching children's educational programmes together, educational success within their extended families and the ripple effect it produces, parent relationship with teachers and the school and if this has a positive or negative impact on schoolwork, and parents having successful friends and family who become commonplace in their children's lives.

Just over half of the fathers admitted to having a negative school experience and lacking literacy skills, so finding a 'comfort zone' around compulsory schoolwork and reading to their children was difficult. None of the fathers believed that their negative experiences has had an impact on their children's ability to learn or succeed at school.

Those fathers who did not regularly read to their children took issue with some of the research findings. They believed that that the low figures for fathers who read to their children does not fully explain the reasons for this. They argued that some fathers are simply too busy trying to make ends meet. They felt it implied a lack of caring among fathers, a kind of lax attitude, and preferring to do other things than applying themselves to read with their children when, in fact, they were actively ensuring their children received assistance from direct family members who understood the school curriculum better than they did, and some even paid for extra tuition when an identified course weakness needed addressing.

Some of the fathers who did shift work agreed with some of the findings, which highlighted the difficulty for some fathers to find the time to read even a bedtime story to their children due to their working patterns. Although they read to their children, it tended to be irregular and dictated by work shift patterns and the need for sleep. However, they took a keen interest in their children's school life by regularly talking to them about this.

These fathers were not surprised that there were no studies detailing the detrimental effects of not reading with your children. They felt that parents and society at large would ridicule any professional body who discounted the value and positive impact of parents contributing to reading or homework.

Past experience of school

It was clear that we had a divide between fathers that could be the key as to whether fathers read to their children or not. The divide seems to be based on whether the fathers' experiences at school were positive or negative.

A clear indicator was that over a quarter of the fathers who attained up to a 'A' level qualification and above seemed to take a more active and direct role in reading with their children. Their experience of school, teacher relationships, and the school curriculum seemed to be rewarding for them, and this attitude has been transferred into the schoolwork with their children. These fathers strongly agreed with the report findings that taking an active part in their children's education, such as reading, would improve their educational success.

However, these fathers were strongly against the studies encouraging reading *Sports Illustrated* or *Golf Illustrated* or talking about football being better than not reading to your children at all. They felt that these studies sent out the wrong message to men. These fathers strongly felt that some fathers who lacked applying themselves when it came to their children's schoolwork should find the time to understand the school curriculum in order to assist and improve their children's academic chances at school. One father admitted to being rubbish at maths whilst at school but spent time in the evening learning some of his daughter's Maths formula to assist her.

The entire group said they knew fathers who really struggled academically. These fathers tended to have experienced a negative schooling environment, so their attitude and confidence towards educational attainment was low, and they found it difficult to separate their past school experiences with their children's modern-day schooling.

The group identified these fathers as sports 'nuts' who lived and breathed football and other sports all season. Their emotions and moods were based on their clubs' successes or failures, and they found it difficult to transfer their energy to the application of homework that had become alien to them. 'Mum will help you,' seemed to be their chosen get-out clause when asked for help from their children. This has, at times, led to tension within these families as football spans nine months of the year and longer if a major summer tournament occurs.

Whilst the group accepted that football was the national sport (there were many heated discussions about their teams' performances during the season), they felt they could draw the line when it came to their love of sport and the need for educational commitment towards their children.

Shift work

By far, the number one factor seeming to hinder fathers from reading with their children are unsocial work patterns, in particular, shift work, whereby fathers are hardly at home due to the long working hours, and when they are at home, they are catching up on their sleep. The phrase, 'Can't see in the morning to can't see at night,' coined by a good friend of mine to explain our fathers' long working hours in the 1960s and 1970s, is still relevant today, as explained by some fathers:

> **Winston:** 'When my kids are at home, I am at work, and when they are at school, I am sleeping. I don't like it, but I have to earn a living and put food on my family's table. It would be nice to help with their homework, but if I'm honest, I'm not comfortable with books. I didn't enjoy school, but it would be nice to have the choice to help them.'

It is fair to say that the professionally qualified fathers I met seemed more likely to work regular nine to five jobs, have more employment protection, and have the ability to take advantage of more flexible hours than semi-skilled and unskilled workers. This flexibility in work patterns means they are able to participate more in their children's educations and are likely to be available during the weekend, whereas lower-skilled workers may work Saturday and/or Sunday to maximise their earning potentials. Winston's experience was echoed by many fathers and went some way to explaining some fathers' low involvement.

The female role

The majority of fathers were not surprised that some studies found mothers tended to be the main readers to children at home. In general, fathers felt their partners and/or wives showed much more patience and involvement, taking twice as long to complete the bedtime story than they did. One father noted, 'My wife allows our children to ask questions during storytime, whereas I do not like being interrupted with questions. I prefer them to wait until I have finished the story, or better still, say goodnight and go to sleep.'

So, fathers admitted that stories should end when the last page had closed, as they did not have the same patience as their partners. What is clear is that mothers were already burdened with multiple tasks at work and in the home, and they still found the time or resources within their extended family and friends to ensure their children kept up with their classmates.

Conclusion

During conversation, many fathers conceded that there seemed to be some correlation between reading to children and success at school. However, they found it difficult to define success in relation to reading alone because they felt many other factors contributed to a child's educational success.

They were impressed with the longevity of some studies, which seemed to link the importance of school qualifications with the attitudes and contributions of parents throughout their children's schooling. The fathers were very aware, due to some of their low earning potentials due to low educational attainment, how not having qualifications could have an impact on future life opportunities and earning potential. This was of concern to fathers across all professions. However, the professional fathers seemed to take more action to ensure their direct involvement.

Three-quarters of the fathers to whom I spoke felt that, due to their culture and extended family links, they identified which family members (tended to be female) who could support their children's reading and other educational needs. For instance, Uncle Ben is good at maths, or Cousin Brenda had a high GSCE English literacy pass last year, so their skills and knowledge would be utilised. In addition, the fathers' experiences of growing up within the education system seemed to have an impact on how comfortable they felt about reading and assisting with their children's curriculum work.

Over a quarter of the fathers had a positive education experience and played an active role in their children's homework, whereas the remainder had a negative experience, so direct participation in homework varied, but the value of other activities – such as visiting the library and having a set time for homework – remained.

Fathers found that their employment patterns could be a barrier to regularly reading with their children, and this was highlighted by irregular shift patterns among the fathers. However, some fathers still took an active role in their children's education in different ways, such as talking about school and accessing paid tutors when necessary.

Of course, the approaches to education are personal and subjective in each and every family, but modern-day apps played much more of a role than just traditional book reading and this added fun to interacting with their children. Families have varying aspirations for their children, and we have to respect this. We believe that as fathers – along with the majority of the population – the issue of education brings up various emotions where parents are concerned.

Some rational and some irrational gossip around local communities, rumours of good and bad schools, league tables, OFSTED inspections, anti-bullying policies, whether grants were maintained, whether private or independent schools were best, statistics on GCSE/'A' level/degree historical grades, and whether there was a good ethnic mix or not. The list used to make a decision seems to be endless.

There was a huge acknowledgement from fathers of their partners' contributions to the organisation and planning of schoolwork and schooling in general, and their dependencies on their partners and/or wives for keeping them up to speed with important dates, such as revision tests and/or exams, gaps in learning, and parent's evenings. 'My wife tells me when and where, and I just do it,' explained one father.

Study after study shows that parental involvement in their children's learning positively affects children's academic performances in both primary and secondary school.

What most fathers were clear about, no matter their profession or how involved they were with their children's education, was that our children will need good qualifications compared to their counterparts to ensure their ethnicity is not a barrier to them when obtaining gainful employment.

Report after report continues to highlight Black boys' educational difficulties and experiences in the school system and boys in general when it comes to picking up a book and reading. Assisting your children with reading and homework is just one element of ensuring success at school. A positive environment for learning at home, parents negotiating a healthy relationship with the school and teachers, extended family input, verbal encouragement, family activities such as visiting libraries, developing a love of books at an early age, and fathers finding a balance between sport and their children's school needs are all a part of the equation, but most important of all is to have fun, to avoid seeing school as a chore.

We posed a lot of questions at the beginning of the chapter, and we hope we have been able to answer some of them, allowing you to think about the topic and how it might affect you as fathers. As we promised earlier in the chapter, we have not lectured you, but let the evidence speak for itself, and you to decide on your next steps.

Putting the Jigsaw Together – Being a Father

"In life, every man has twin obligations – obligations to his family, to his parents, to his wife and children; and he has an obligation to his people, his community, his country."

– Nelson Mandela

Who better than Nelson Mandela to provide the closing quotation for my book? His powerful words encapsulate the challenges we face as men of colour living in the UK. Mandela's words of wisdom provide us with a clarity of thought that internationally translate around the world what he believes should be our focus and responsibilities within our life.

He understood the physical and spiritual interconnectedness of men in our family and community. Perhaps Mandela wanted to help us to re-connect with systems that benefit and give us a sense of purpose, belonging and recognition, if we seek it out, rather than concentrate on what, at times, can seem like a 'dog eat dog' system that we struggle to survive in.

Perhaps we struggle partly because we are trying to function in a system that is not our true nature, and why statistics continue to highlight terrible outcomes for us men in the Northern hemisphere.

We do not always realise, but our DNA is family, community, wife, partner, son, children, brotherhood, friendships, fatherhood and work. These are the things that can help us regain our sense of belonging, connection, purpose and contentment in life.

So this final chapter concentrates on us being able to self-reflect and understand our place in our community and the values that we hold dear to us. Values that can become lost over time but can be reignited by meeting and talking to other fathers to keep the torch burning.

Understanding yourself and what makes you tick is the starting point, not only in fatherhood but in all relationships you have in life. I truly believe that every man in Britain should attend some type of counselling or personal development sessions to really get to know himself, what makes him tick, and reflect on how he lives his life. This is because so many men either consciously or unconsciously fall into a subjective masculine 'typecast' of how they think a man should think and behave, and this can, at times, be way off the mark from what their families and partners actually need from them. Someone once said, 'You have to choose between what the world expects of you and what you expect of yourself.' This message runs so true in our community, where research shows that so many of our young men are either in prison, in mental institutions, or they are unemployed for the long term. However, not all of us have fallen by the wayside. So many fathers have spoken about the important decisions they took whilst growing up to ensure they did not become another statistic and the importance of using their experiences to guide their children through the difficult times they are sure to encounter.

The world will always stereotype individuals and groups of people in a positive or negative way – that's just the way the world works, a form of divide and conquer that pits people from different backgrounds against each other, and it will continue to long after we have gone. However, these stereotypes can become dangerous if you start to believe what is being said or written about you or your group, and you start to act in the negative manner expected of you. The day you decide not to fit into all the destructive stereotypes expected of you is the day you really hold the power to your destiny. You will need to start to value yourself in thought and behaviour, and in turn, you will expect more from yourself in life, and so will others. Set goals and values around education, employment, and building a strong network of support within your community. I have spoken to so many fathers who admit that the journey to understanding and wanting to understand who they are, were difficult but rewarding journeys. One father quoted Michael Jackson's song 'Man in the Mirror' as the words seemed to ring true for him: 'If you want to make the world a better place take a look at yourself and make that change.' If you haven't already done so, it is time for us as fathers to start looking in the mirror and asking ourselves some serious questions. Am I the best father and husband and/or partner that I can be? If not, what can I do to improve the situation for the good of my family and myself? Here is some feedback from fathers, both young and old, that has helped them improve their understanding of themselves and the importance of fatherhood over the years.

- Taking responsibility for our actions and finding out who we really are by understanding what makes us tick, what triggers different emotions within us – such as happy, sad, angry, and/or tearful – is a powerful weapon because we start to take control of our emotional responses. Rather than emotionally closing down and not talking to friends, families, or wives to release our frustrations and share our burdens, it can be uplifting and a big relief when others show their concern and give us ideas about how to deal with our problems.

- Decide what your goals are in life and try complimenting them with the needs of your family. Some fathers end up growing apart from their families and partners because they did not communicate their goals properly, as families and partners can be great sources of support.

- Understand that your mind can be your greatest obstacle or asset and start to believe in yourself; believe in your ability to achieve even when people and society may tell you that you will never succeed. Develop a thick skin.

- Try thinking outside the box into which you and society have placed you as this will allow you to release the shackles that hold you back and plan your future.

- It's okay if your son wants to become or a ballet dancer or your daughter an engineer – it's not a reflection of your masculinity; honest!

- Successful people, including fathers, see the positives and opportunities in negative situations and make these situations work for them and not against them.

- Know your strengths and weaknesses better than your enemies; your inner fight is not with them but with yourself.

- Work out your moral boundaries, what you will and will not do as a matter of principle and communicate these to your children. Build a positive image of yourself, show confidence, and others will see the same in you. If you have moral boundaries, it is likely your children will have these, too.

- Show humility to others rather than have a big ego as egos are about selfishness, and humility is about modesty, and being humble can open so many doors in life.

- Learn to be calm in adversity to allow clear thinking and clear decision-making as this can often get you out of trouble.

- Respect women who cross your path and categorically denounce all disrespectful terminologies and music with excessive sexualised images towards our women. Remember your daughters are also affected.

If you could achieve half of these goals, it would mean you are no longer a victim of your situation but a master of it. Being a victim can be a paralysing state of body and mind and difficult to get out of. I find that minority groups all around the world can display this trait, and it can be a powerless and debilitating state of mind. Being a victim does not equip you with a blueprint to get out of the situation you are in but having clear goals does. So many fathers and grandfathers I have met were not initially successful in their lives or in fatherhood, but they made decisions along the way to change their mindset and take charge of their lives, and if they have not already done so, it's not too late. All the examples I've highlighted are elements of what makes them the fathers they are today. Some of the fathers would like you to know that once you have a blueprint for your personal development, you can then develop a blueprint for life with your family and your community.

Irrelevant of age or culture, every father I have met either in a planned manner or through chance, I have asked the same question: what is it like to be a father of colour, given the negative press you experience? This question has driven me throughout the process of writing my book because our capacity to parent has a direct impact on the happiness of our wives, partners and ex-partners, children, and extended and immediate families. How the community perceives us and how we perceive ourselves are determining factors to our existence as fathers. Whether our children are brought up to be well-balanced and successful individuals in adult life or troubled individuals who struggle to fit into the rules and structure of society largely depends on how we as parents conduct ourselves and live our lives in front of our children.

What I have learned from listening to fathers is that there is no one approach to fatherhood that fits all. We all have different upbringings, influences, and attitudes towards parenting and disciplining. However, through my journey, I learned that core components to fatherhood exist that can form a blueprint to improving our understanding and enhance our parenting skills. A key component to creating this blueprint is to be clear on your core values as a father. Your values are your guiding principles in life. What are your core values? What do you live by? A father said to me, 'A person who believes in nothing will fall for anything.' This has always stuck with me when I think about the values I want to pass onto my children. Your core values will give them the foundations throughout their childhood and adulthood.

We do not expect you to embrace all of what is written here, but we do hope some of our ideas will appeal to you, and you will find the confidence or courage to put some of them into practice.

An enduring relationship from child to adult

Almost all the men I met were clear that one of the main components to fatherhood is setting a good example for their children. By demonstrating good behaviours of a good role model, showing strong morals and values and a sense of family belonging, it is likely that your children will follow in your footsteps. If you are clear about your blueprint or approach for bringing up your children, they will be clear about what you expect from them. We are the best role models our children can have, and we can positively influence a generation of future adults.

This leads us on to one of the enduring arts of fatherhood: embracing your children even when they have grown up and moved on. To keep the foundations of your generations going, you need to communicate with your children in a positive way when they become adults so that they will want to come to visit you long after they have left home. They are now adults, after all, and making their way in life, but they should still have a desire to visit the old man. If they feel that a visit to your home will be more of a lecture on how they should be running their lives, they will keep visits down to a minimum. Subtly planting seeds rather than making unreasonable demands is an approach that seems to be more successful in later parent-adult relationships. As one grandfather explained:

> **Verol:** 'There is an art to communicating with your grown-up children. A one-way lecture is no longer acceptable, but a two-way, adult conversation seems to be the key, and you can also pass on some advice without them feeling put upon.'

If your family and friends (both male and female) are a positive reflection of you, your children will grow to and see such positive role models as an everyday occurrence in your household. Below are a few caveats I wanted to add before drawing this book to a close. Some things to ponder on as you explore the depth of fatherhood.

Showing your family unit love and protection

Both fathers and grandfathers felt frustrated with men who neglect their family duties, and this can, at times, reflect badly on our gender. A responsible man protects his family from the threats of the outside world. Providing your family with stability, emotional support, and financial protection came high on the list of ways men felt they should protect their families. As previously mentioned in the book, and to what Nelson Mandela's quotation alluded, a man will be judged by society on his work and how he protects and treats his family. This is partly why some Black men have gained a negative image in society (though there are also historical and psychological reasons) because if you cannot care and look after your own, for whom can you care? Unless we are unable to take care of ourselves (physically and mentally) as men, we should honour our responsibilities towards our children and partners or ex-partners because if we do not, society has every right to feel aggrieved with us because it has to clear up the messes of our broken homes.

School days are the best days of your life

This is a reoccurring theme amongst most groups I spoke to. More fathers need to have a positive attitude towards education and encourage their children to continue into higher education. The term 'school days are the best days of your life' has two meanings. Firstly, children and teenagers are exposed to educational establishments that help them open their minds and develop their intellectual capacities on a daily basis. Secondly, learning is the biggest gift you can give to your children, as it determines their future careers, lifestyles, and financial independence rather than live in poverty, and as already mentioned, whether you have any control over the hours you work and the amount of leave you obtain to spend with your family.

My mum used to say, 'Stay in education until you have a grey beard.' I didn't understand at the time, but she said it so many times that it stuck with me. I think I took her a little too seriously as I continue to work and study to this day to improve my skill set and opportunities. Fathers have spoken about similar experiences with their parents, aunts, or uncles who have tried to encourage them to stay in education and gain their qualifications. We know that some fathers' experiences at school were negative, but their negative past in school should not affect their children's educational chances and the parents' encouragement towards it. We cannot express enough how important qualifications are in this technological age in which we live. Look at the job advertisements, and you'll see that a pre-requisite for applying for so many jobs today is some type of qualification. If your child does not have the qualification needed for the job, forget applying! So, pass the same message on to your children and try to encourage them to stay in college, university, or training if possible, by using the tack that one father has used successfully for years. He advised his children if they stayed in education, they could live at home rent-free, but if they decided to work, they would have to pay rent and contribute to the utility bills. Needless to say, they decided to continue studying.

Respecting women's ability to give life

If you have attended the birth of your child (it's allowed nowadays, but it is not for the faint-hearted), you will witness the amazing power of nature and the determination of women to manage the pain and give life all in the same breath. In centuries gone by, the ability of women to give life and rear children were revered in communities, but I fear this is no longer the case.

Unfortunately, issues such as Britain having the highest teenage pregnancy rate in Europe and the world of work are seen as more important than child-rearing, leading to the downgrading of childbirth and childcare. Of course, there are many other reasons why childbirth and child-rearing has been downgraded, such as the impact of work becoming all-important or a necessity in our lives and the still-prevailing Victorian attitude that children should be seen and not heard has meant that society no longer views children as an investment in our future but as an irritant. In addition, the financial pressure for most women to return to work to make ends meet, but when they do return to work, they are criticised for leaving their children. As men, we can forget the amazing gift of life given to us by our own mothers and then our children by our partners as we struggle through the day-to-day rat race.

A father once told me, 'As men, we need to remember those days in the delivery room, our emotional connections with our partners, and the new lives we hold in our hands, the exhilaration we felt when we were told by the midwife, "It's a girl," or "It's a boy."' He explained that we should hold on and never forget that special feeling when nature provided us with the gift of life. So, even during or after arguments with our partners and when things are looking bleak, we should try to remember the true gifts our partners have given us: our children.

Being at peace within yourself and the ability to self-reflect
This follows the first topic I wrote about in this chapter, understanding yourself and your place in the family and community. As an ex-counsellor for children and young people, part of my role was to enable them to reflect on the difficulties in their lives to make sense of them and possibly resolve them. I found that my clients who were able to take a step back and talk openly, no matter how difficult, about their actions were the ones more likely to resolve their difficulties. Having the ability to honestly reflect

on how you have dealt with situations or people in your life and explore whether your reaction was the right or wrong approach is an important life skill to learn.

The gift of self-reflection is a powerful self-awareness tool not many adults find easy to face or do. As human beings, we are able to rationalise our world and the ways we behave. Therefore, we also can change the way we behave if we choose to. I have found that the people who developed ways to reflect on their actions are the ones more likely to lead a fulfilling life because they do not make the same mistakes repeatedly.

If you know that you have a destructive temper and continually put your wife down, lose friends or family members, do you sweep it under the carpet though you know you were in the wrong? We all make mistakes in life, but those who can reflect and say, 'That was wrong, and I am going to seek help to change,' are the people who find inner peace. They are willing to self-reflect, no matter how painful it might be and try to change their behaviours. Some fathers I met had unresolved issues that caused them and their families a great deal of pain. Their partners were hanging in there because they were committed to the relationship and wanted their men to get better. However, these issues do not just go away. As men, we are very good at suppressing our feelings, but unless we can make peace with ourselves, we will find it difficult to make peace with our families. Whatever your story, life is difficult enough with the pressures of modern-day living continually trying to pound you into submission. Those dads who do not resolve their inner demons are the ones that life eventually breaks down at a heavy cost to their families. To give yourself a fighting chance, a chance to be the best father you can, try to find inner peace.

The penny drops: appreciating your parents

How many times have you found yourself lecturing your children and hear your parents' words coming out of your mouth? Isn't it an odd feeling as growing up, you vowed never to be like them as you listened to one lecture following another? You realised then, no matter your differences with your parents' upbringing, some of what they said must have been right. The job our parents tried to do, whether successfully or less so, was to transmit the strong values and discipline they learned as children. They didn't always use the right methods, but their intention was to try to send us along our ways into adulthood with strong characters and a sense of right and wrong. Quite a few fathers confessed to thanking their mothers and apologising for giving them hell by continually getting into trouble as children. So, decisions by their parents to quell their activities were to protect them from harm. They now understand that their cavalier approaches might have placed them in a lot of danger.

Staying or running away

There are two types of running away men tend to do after an argument. Firstly, we storm out in furious rages, slamming the doors behind us. Some men spoke about needing the space to cool down, and invariably, this is the group that returns after a few minutes or hours, makeup with their partners, and life goes on. Secondly, rather than return after an argument or incident, some of us permanently run away, leaving the responsibilities of home and the family life behind. The reasons can, at times, be complex and outside of this book's remit. When talking to a few men who have left, they admitted to having been brought up with absent fathers. Not having a male or father role model whilst growing meant they did not experience how men dealt with the pressures of relationships and fatherhood. There was no model to follow and no one to guide them. Leaving home seemed like the only alternative when dealing with the pressure of family life and fatherhood, as that is exactly what their dads had done.

However, they also admitted there comes a time when you can no longer hide or run from your demons. You need to work on your personal problems and accept and seek professional help, if need be, for the sake of your children and partners – if she will have you back, that is. It is unfair to expect her to provide for the family both financially and emotionally, day in and day out, with minimal help from you. Our women are intelligent, beautiful, and strong, but our help is also needed to ease the burden on them.

Again, Mandela's words of wisdom remain relevant to this topic and all fathers' experiences throughout my book. Whether you have a male role model or not, we can embrace him as our honorary grandfather; allow his words of wisdom to occupy our minds in times of need in our desire to be the best man we can be. Our newfound confidence and connections to other fathers allows us to talk about the issues that bind us together and gain insight into our lived experience. We no longer have to suffer in silence, and in doing so, we become less invisible.

About the Author

Kenny Harry was born in East London to Dominican parents and is a father of two children, Aaliyah and Terrel. He has seven brothers and sisters living in London, Essex, Sheffield, and Dominica.

Kenny has a diploma in youth and community work and counselling, BSc (hons) degree in social policy and research, a post-graduate certificate in health and social care management and a master's degree in social work. Kenny previously worked as a qualified youth worker with children and young people, a counsellor mainly working with young men with anger management, healthy relationships and sexual health issues, a mentor coordinator training social workers to mentor looked after children, a manager working with care leavers, and a counsellor for NSPCC.

At present, Kenny works as an Independent social worker for a local authority; Independent work assessing potential foster carers and a fostering panel member.

Kenny first became aware of the need for a parenting book for fathers living in Britain due to fathers seeking advice from him on a number of fatherhood and relationship issues. All of the books he recommended at the time were American in origin, and he saw the need for a book that highlighted Fathers' UK experiences having to manoeuvre what tends to be a hostile environment towards them.

He has devoted his life working with children and young people, believing that all young people have untapped talent, and given the right encouragement and direction, can fulfil their potentials.

Conscious Dreams
P U B L I S H I N G

Transforming diverse writers
into successful published authors

 www.consciousdreamspublishing.com

 authors@consciousdreamspublishing.com

Let's connect